ACTUALLY FUNNY POLITICALLY CORRECT JOKES

ACTUALLY FUNNY POLITICALLY CORRECT JOKES

MARTY FIELDS

Published by:
Wilkinson Publishing Pty Ltd
ACN 006 042 173
Level 4, 2 Collins Street
Melbourne, Vic 3000
Ph: 03 9654 5446
www.wilkinsonpublishing.com.au

A catalogue record for this book is available from the National Library of Australia

Planned date of publication: 08-2019
Title: Actually Funny Politically Correct Jokes
ISBN(s): 9781925927009: Printed – Paperback

Design by Spike Creative Pty Ltd
Ph: (03) 9427 9500
spikecreative.com.au

Printed in Australia by Griffin Press, a part of Ovato

DEDICATION

This book is dedicated to my family, Jenny and Hayley, and my Mum and Dad and Grandfather who taught me to be funny. Where would we be without having people to look up to?

Also my mates in the industry away from comedy, Ken Murdoch, Syd Heylen Jnr, Wayne and Kate Kermond. And my mates in comedy at the Comics Lounge in Melbourne, the owners and the acts. You said this book wasn't possible. Maybe you'll be proven right but I've had a crack!

FOREWORD

Welcome to a heap of harmless laughs. I'm sure you're going to enjoy them. But just because they're clean, doesn't mean they're not funny. I've scoured my collection for great inoffensive gags. I reckon these are rippers, and I've been doing this comedy caper for over forty years.

Jokes like to poke fun at people, things, situations and places. But having fun at someone else's expense can stop it being fun. So here's a collection of gags that I'm pretty sure won't upset anybody.

A lot of comics have given up trying to be politically correct because it's hard to please everybody and the rules keep changing. My response to that is,

1. you'll never please everybody and you'll go crazy trying to, and

2. this job requires you to keep up with an ever-changing marketplace.

The comedy landscape has changed, no doubt. But with a little restructuring of gags, and deciding if an offensive joke is worth the grief, you can still survive in comedy.

I like to think I've always worked pretty clean so the current trend isn't such a leap for me. I never saw the merit in shock humour. I'd rather be witty.

Although with all of that being said, I'm often surprised at how some people find offence when none was intended. None is intended here. They're just jokes. You'll be OK.

But thanks for trusting me.

Cheers,

Marty

ACTUALLY FUNNY POLITICALLY CORRECT JOKES

I said to the Gym instructor, 'Can you teach me to do the splits?' He said, 'How flexible are you?' I said, 'I can't make Tuesdays.'

....

I told my wife she should embrace her mistakes.

She hugged me.

....

WAITER: Would you like Parmesan cheese on your meal?

ME: Yes please.

WAITER: Say when.

ME: Well, now before I start makes the most sense.

....

I'm throwing a ball for my dog.
But she refuses to wear the gown
and tiara.

....

I found out why when you're scuba
diving, to get in the water you always
fall backwards off the side of the boat.
Because if you fall forwards, you're still
in the boat.

....

I just realised my car has a parking sensor.
When I reverse too close to something it
makes a banging, crunching noise.

....

People think the word 'queue' is just 'q'
followed by four silent letters. But those
letters are not silent. They're just waiting
for their turn.

....

A 62-year-old American woman has
failed in an attempt to swim from Cuba
to Florida. She lasted 43 hours into the
shark infested ocean swim before having
to retire due to cramping and over 60
jellyfish stings to her torso, face, lips and
eyes. She did however break the record for
the worst possible way to spend 43 hours.

....

I don't like Aldi. They have brands that are similar to normal but not quite the same. In the cereal aisle I saw a box of Ordinary K.

....

ME: 'Loud noises scare camels.'

WIFE: *(now whispering)* 'Get it out of the house!'

....

My wife says the reason our lovemaking is so bad is because I'm easily distracted.

Ah well, back to it I suppose.

....

There's a mobile phone that fires bullets, although you can't shoot anyone in an underground car park or a lift.

....

The world's best darts player has died. The cause of death was the world's worst darts player.

....

At the shopping centre I watched a woman take her baby into the baby change room but when she came out she had the same baby so they should tell people it's out of order or something.

....

They should stock ATMs better.
I went to four different ones and they
all said 'insufficient funds'.

....

Nothing is made in Australia anymore.
I just bought a TV and it says 'Built
in antenna'. I don't even know where
that is.

....

How many opticians does it take to change
a light bulb?
Is it one or two? One... or two?

....

I bet pillow fights used to go for a lot less
time in the Stone Age.

....

At the chemist I asked the pharmacist
if they had some cream for my rash.
She said, 'Where is it?'
I said, 'How would I know? It's your shop.'

....

I was a very skinny kid. One time my dad
took me into a pool hall and they chalked
up my head.

....

I stayed in a really old hotel. They sent me a wake up letter.

....

I was staying at the Sofitel. I went up to reception. I said, 'I've had a few drinks and I've forgotten what room I'm in.'
He said, 'No problem. This is the "lobby".'

....

My problem is I have just enough money to get into trouble tonight but not enough money to make bail.

....

Don't waste your money on deodorant.
If you don't buy it pretty soon people will just give it to you for free.

....

If you're just starting as a getaway car driver, trust me, work out how to put your seat back BEFORE the bank robber jumps in the car.

....

The Magician pulls a rabbit out of his hat and makes doves appear from a handkerchief.
ZOOKEEPER: 'And the penguin in your backpack. Hand it over.'

....

As I walk through the valley of the Shadow of Death, I remind myself that you can't always trust Google Maps.

....

I remember the first time I posted a selfie on social media and people told me to 'get well soon'.

....

I don't understand why clothes are so expensive. I shouldn't have to pay this much to not be naked. People should pay ME to not be naked.

....

My Grandfather used to take five showers a day. When he died, as a tribute to his cleanliness, the entire funeral procession went through a car wash.

....

I used to play in a metal band. Heavy metal bands have intense names like 'Megadeath' and 'Rigor mortis'. We weren't that intense. We were called 'Sore Leg'. Then we changed it to 'Paper Cut'. As we were walking out of the pawn shop we changed our name to 'Accapella'.

....

Have you ever woken up on the wrong side of the bed? I'm like, 'How'd I get under here?'

....

I was changing a light bulb, so I used my step-ladder because I don't get on with my real ladder.

....

I saw in paper our local RSL is looking for a new treasurer. I rang them. I said, 'Didn't you just hire a new treasurer a month ago?' They said, 'That's the one we're looking for.'

....

Some guy broke into our house and tried to steal our TV, but it was too heavy so he stole the TV remote control. Now he drives by and changes channels on us.

....

I think a bad place for a fire would be the factory where they make those trick birthday candles. 'OK, fellas, we're done here. Oh, come on! Alright everybody, make another wish.'

....

I bought a fifty-dollar pen because I lose pens all the time and I'm sick of not caring.

....

I got pulled over by the cops. I said,
'I'm taking my wife to the hospital.
She's OD'd on weight loss pills.'
He says, 'I don't see anyone else in the car.'
I said, 'I'm too late!'

....

I was sitting at home having a drink with
my wife and she said, 'I love you.'

I said, 'Is that you or the wine talking?'
She said, 'It's me talking... to the wine.'

....

My dog won first prize at the dog show
today so we all came home and drank
champagne out of the toilet.

....

I was the youngest in my family.
I'm an only child.

....

Vincent Van Gough cut off his ear and
sent it to the woman who had left him.
How romantic. If I sent a body part to every
girl that dumped me, I'd just be a toe.

....

I bought 200 kilos of steel wool.
I'm knitting a garage.

....

Did you hear Qantas are expanding Jetstar's international operations? Good idea because if there's one thing better than having no food or leg room, it's having it for longer flights.

....

Werribee Zoo's new gorilla enclosure has been breached by professional climbers who were invited in to test its escapability. As a result the enclosure's walls have been enhanced making them unclimbable. You can visit the climbers daily but don't get too close. They seem angry.

....

Dutch rail passengers are being offered plastic bags to use in 'an emergency' on new trains that are not fitted with toilets. I wouldn't want to be a porter at a station in Holland. 'Can I take your bags, sir?'

....

An ambulance driver who lost his job said he was discriminated against because he is short, despite patients repeatedly falling off his end of the stretcher.

....

The Spiderman burglar has struck again. Police say the best way of protecting your home is to treat your window sills with surface spray. And while not condoning the Spiderman's actions, police said they did have to concede he was doing a great job of keeping away the Human Fly.

....

A guy at my gig last night was grumpy right through the show. I said to him, 'What's wrong?' He said, 'I hate my job.' I said, 'You hate your job? There's a support group for that. It's called 'everybody'. We meet at the bar each night.'

....

I like to bet. My oldest daughter turned seven on a Saturday so I threw her a birthday party at our local TAB. All the kids are crying. I'm like, 'Calm down, I'll pay you back.'

....

Rosella has announced they are sacking 300 workers at their tomato sauce factory. According to a company spokesperson, those employees who refuse to leave the plant will be shaken and smacked on the bottom till they come out.

....

Why does the Pope have all those guards and bullet proof vehicles? If he's afraid to go to heaven, what chance do we have?

Have you got a complaint about the tax department? Call their convenient hotline: 1800 AUDITME.

The founder of Hoyts Cinemas died today. His funeral will be held Thursday at 1.20, 3.40, 5.50 and 7pm.

The health department has just approved pills that make help you lose weight by making you feel full. The recommended dosage is 5,000 pills a day.

I know I'm getting fat when I get in the bathtub and the water in the toilet goes up.

I put a steering lock on my old Datsun 120Y which was dumb because someone broke in, left the car, and stole the lock.

I rang the Home Shopping Network.
The operator said, 'Can I help you?'
I said, 'No, I'm just looking.'

....

Pregnancy is amazing. To think you can
create a human just with the things you
have around the house.

....

The man who invented the IQ test has
died when his car travelling ten k's an
hour was hit by a train doing 90 k's
an hour.

....

The founder of Krispy Kreme Donuts
has died. He went peacefully. Apparently
his eyes just glazed over.

....

My friend has a tattoo of a pocket on
his hip. I asked him why. He said inside
it he has a tattoo of his car keys.

....

Aaron is the worst name. It's the first
name in The Baby Name Book. How lazy
can your parents be? You're lucky your
name's not Copyright.

....

Call a girl once and she doesn't call back, it's possible she hasn't got the message. Call her 20 times and she still hasn't called back, it's you who hasn't got the message.

....

Everyone's got caller ID. I'm waiting for caller IQ.

....

NASA has announced that the sun is only 4.2 billion years old. It just looks older because it's spent so much time in the sun.

....

My cousin, from time to time, puts on her wedding dress. Not because she's sentimental. She just gets way behind with her laundry.

....

Ever go to a drive-in movie, get drunk and pass out and wake up in middle of a trash and treasure market? I sold my spare tyre for ten bucks.

....

I just want a girl who will like me for who I am pretending to be.

....

I'm not sure about Hungry Jacks.
How good could can the joint be if the
guy who owns it is hungry? I'd prefer
Big Fat Happy Jacks.

....

Brisbane is confusing to drive around.
A Queensland cop pulls me over. I said,
'You only pulled me over because I've
got Victorian number plates.' He said,
'No, we've been pulling over every car
driving down this footpath.'

....

I went to buy a candle holder, but they
didn't have one so I bought a cake.

....

I drink so much when Jack Daniels
does his tax return he lists me as a
dependent.

....

They say *Sesame Street* is educational but
the Cookie Monster has been living there
for 40 years and he's still dumb as a rock.

....

My auntie is old. Her childhood illness
was the plague.

....

I prove the theory that speedos are a privilege not a right.

....

Olympic athletes are all moaning about how we disrespect the amount of training they have to do. The early mornings, the cold water. Whadda they want, a medal?

....

My company put out a suggestion box and offered a hundred-dollar reward to any employee who came up with an idea how to save the company money. I wrote, 'Make the reward fifty bucks.'

....

A poem:

I don't like my neighbour.
I throw tomatoes at him.
Tomatoes are soft and don't really hurt,
But these do, they're still in the tin.

....

You can always tell a good hotel by how fluffy the towels are in the rooms. The Last hotel I stayed in was magnificent. I could hardly get my case shut.

....

I bought a box of chocolates in London. The cashier said, 'That'll be ten pounds.' I'm like, 'Rub it in, why don't you?'

....

The great thing about gangs is they car pool.

....

Out of all the geniuses who make smart phones, I want to meet the one who said, 'Wait. Let's make the charger cords shorter!'

....

When I delete an App on my iPhone all the other apps start shaking like they're scared they'll be next.

....

I'm too old now. A girl said to me, 'Do you know what I'd like to see you in?' I said, 'What?' She said '1987'.

....

We've just had a lunar eclipse in Australia. So spare a thought for all the werewolves who got stuck with just sideburns and a goatee.

....

There was a brawl outside the Lygon Street restaurant strip. Cops subdued the crowd with freshly cracked pepper spray.

....

95% of women say they don't like men who wear leather pants. That works out because 95% of men who wear leather pants don't like women.

....

If you drive to a nightclub and get too drunk to drive home don't call a cab, call a tow-truck. It'll cost a little more but your car will be there at home when you wake up.

....

Police are treating a fire in a scrap metal yard as suspicious. If it was arson it's an impressive job. Have you ever tried to set fire to scrap metal?

....

Australians are buying an injectable tanning drug so loaded with side-effects that it's been banned in most countries in the world including Australia. It's amazing how the people buying this stuff are cool about using a banned tanning injection yet too scared to just sun-bake.

....

In the latest Galaxy poll results, the Morrison Government's approval rating has fallen to a new low. But the party spin doctors were quick to point out that they're still above a root canal and fleas.

....

Two Irish guys are trying to cross Antarctica on a sled pulled by a kite. They'd use sled dogs but that's what sober people would do.

....

The government plans to crack down on charity collectors by making them wear name tags. This is great news, not only for genuine charities, but also for the owners of 'Fake Name Tags R Us'.

....

Formula One legends McLaren are finally making cars for everyday use. On the downside they cost $7 million but on the positive, you can get them serviced in under 8 seconds.

....

Lady Gaga is coming back to Australia. Gaga is so famous even babies know her name.

....

Prospective buskers in Melbourne are having to audition in front of three Melbourne City Council employees before being allowed to perform. This proves the theory that everyone is an expert on two jobs: their own and show business.

....

The remaining Beatles are releasing yet another song using newly discovered pre-recorded John Lennon vocals called 'We're not home. Leave a message after the beep'.

....

My friend is a hoon driver who's been arrested so many times he has burnout.

....

I took a bus from Perth to Melbourne. Two days in some people were passing round a joint.
I took out my deodorant to pass that around too.

....

It's surprisingly hard to play pool in a pool. The balls slowly roll down to the deep end and the chalk goes all gooey.

....

A blues singer died and his tombstone read, 'Didn't wake up this morning...'

....

A YouTube clip of a guy with chicken pox has gone viral.

....

Leaked documents show George W. Bush prepared for a visit from the Dali Lama by covering the floor with newspaper and buying a bag of carrots.

....

Watching weightlifting is really slow. Pick it up! It's weightlift, not wait... lift.

....

The man who invented the album cover in the late 1930s has died. The details of his life are printed on his inner sleeve.

....

Scientists have fertilised a human egg with rabbit DNA. They're hoping to create a guy with a lucky foot.

....

Just got an email telling me I've won a dozen cans of tinned meat but I think it's just spam.

....

I failed a Health and Safety course at work today. One of the questions was: 'In the event of a fire, what steps would you take?' I said 'Really big ones.'

....

If I had fifty cents for every time someone said I was bad at maths I'd have eighty cents.

....

I like Indian food but only from the waist up.

....

A girl yelled at me in the street, 'Oh my God, you are so hot. I love you!' It's true. If you don't believe me you can ask Hugh Jackman who was right behind me.

....

A kangaroo was filmed trying to mate with a parked BMW convertible and it caused $8,000 damage to the car. But a BMW sitting around with its top down is just asking for it.

....

Despite repeated warnings from authorities, some Australians are mortgaging their houses to send money to the Nigerian fraudsters. The Government is now investigating how these Australians were smart enough to own their own houses in the first place.

....

A man who murdered two fellow inmates while serving a long sentence in a psychiatric hospital has been sentenced to a long sentence in the same psychiatric hospital. That'll teach him.

....

Palaeontologists have discovered that stone hand axes were invented 300,000 years earlier than previously thought. It seems they were used by our African ancestors 'Homo Erectus' who carried the hand axes for protection against Neolithic bullies who made fun of their name, 'Homo Erectus'.

....

$200 million of the stimulant drug cocaine was discovered in a shipment of lawnmowers. Police became suspicious when two gardeners mowed Royal Melbourne Golf Course in eight minutes.

....

Australia's Mathias Cormann has been honoured by being named the 'World's Best Finance Minister' at the Global Finance Minister of the Year Awards. Another major prize handed out on the night was 'Most Boring Awards Function' won by the Global Finance Minister of the Year awards.

....

Winx swept the prize pool at the Racehorse of the Year awards, racing's version of the Logies. She won horse of the year, sprinter of the year and most popular racehorse. 'Awards aren't everything', the horse said, 'Although it's nice to be recognised.' Winx's main rival at the awards, Happy Clapper, walked away empty-hoofed. When asked for a comment the gelding said, 'I left my comment on the red carpet as we came in.'

....

Meatloaf sang at the AFL Grand Final. He performed his hits 'Took the Words Right Out of my Mouth' and 'Bat out of Hell' plus he planned to sing them in tune. If you've ever seen Meatloaf live, you'll know that two out of three ain't bad.

....

A koala got hit by a car and became stuck in the front of the vehicle. He was carried nearly 4km before the driver realised he was stuck there. Police helped remove the koala from the bumper bar and radiator and he waddled off with a few cuts and bruises. Experts said he was probably on his way to mate. I bet his girlfriend wouldn't have been too impressed. 'You're late! Don't tell me you got picked up in that bar and grill again.'

....

Dog urine is being used in China as a hair loss treatment for men. I bet the hard part is to get the dog to go on the bald spot.

....

It's always great when a hotel operator asks you, 'Is he a guest at our hotel?' 'No, he's just driving by the building. Hop over the counter, run out and flag him down for me, would ya?'

....

I just fell off my step ladder. I got so mad I told it, 'You're not my real ladder!'

....

Once you hate someone, everything they do is offensive. 'Look at him over there. Eating that yoghurt like he owns the place.'

....

Everything seems funnier when you're not allowed to laugh.

....

'Mate, that guy just called you a thief!' 'Right, that's it! Hold my jacket and his wallet.'

....

There should be a way to tell someone their breath stinks without offending them. 'I'm bored. Let's go brush your teeth.'

....

I travel a lot so I rent a lot of cars. I'm always in unfamiliar cars. I've been known to travel a long way with the emergency brake on. That doesn't say a lot for me, but says even less for the emergency brake. They shouldn't call it an emergency brake. They should call it a 'Make the car smell weird' lever.

....

When I walk through the city people try and hand me fliers. When someone hands me a flier, what they're really saying is, 'Here, you throw this away.'

....

I've come up with this new game show based on *Who Wants to Be a Millionaire*, but the twist is we use real millionaires risking their own money. Rather than win, they lose money every time they get an answer wrong. It's called 'Who Used to be a Millionaire'.

....

In America, they're putting wedding chapels in Target stores. Wedding chapels in Target? Like the return lines aren't long enough already?

....

At our holiday home we had a lot of trees on the property so my wife buys me a chainsaw. But it's electric. With a 15-metre cord and I don't have an extension lead. 15 metres. So that means I've pretty much gotta get the trees to come to me. Outside our back door we have a perfect 14-metre semicircle clearing.

....

I used to be scared of pretty girls until one confessed they were just as scared of me.

....

I used to work at a carnival cleaning the mirrors in the house of mirrors. By the time I was finished I was lost. That was an awful job. But you know what was worse? Having to watch yourself all day doing that awful job.

....

I'm not too smart. I ran out of petrol outside a massage parlour waiting for the red light to change.

....

If genius is 1% inspiration, and 99% perspiration, then my cab driver must be frickin' Einstein.

....

Did I already do my déjà vu joke?

....

Horse whisperers whisper in a horse's ear and the horse goes, 'OK cool'.

Chinese horse whisperers whisper in a horse's ear and that horse whispers in another horse's ear and that horse whispers in another horse's ear...

....

My father was a man of few words.
I remember he used to say to me, 'Son...'

....

I have a hobby. I collect empty bottles,
which sounds so much better than
'alcoholic'.

....

Just came back from Kalgoorlie. Nothing
out there. Long straight roads. My mate
lives there. His wife left him and he saw
her walking away for five days.

....

How come if you scream in a library
everyone stares at you, but if you scream
on a plane everyone joins in?

....

I bought a bag of plain rolls for two
bucks. And you can get the same rolls but
with sesame seeds and they're also two
bucks. Know what that means? Sesame
seeds cost nothing. But somewhere some
idiot's farming them. That idiot was my
uncle. Uncle Vince. Or as I called him,
Uncle Centrelink.

....

I went into the book shop. I said to the guy, 'I'm looking for a book called "How to deal with rejection without killing someone"... do you have it?'

....

I rang the local swimming pool. I said, 'Is this the local swimming pool?'

They said, 'That depends where you're calling from.'

....

I quit my job at the helium gas factory. I refused to be spoken to in that tone of voice.

....

Our power went out in our house and my wife was freaked out but I said, 'Relax, we'll party like it's 1799.' Which I thought was kind of cute but she really got into the spirit. 'Great idea! Everything we do has to have taken place in 1799. We'll dress up in formal costumes and light candles and...' I said, 'Whoa, hold on. It's 1799. You don't get to vote.'

....

I have a dog named Segue. And speaking of dogs...

....

My auntie was crushed by a piano.
Her funeral was very low key. B Flat.
I can't leave you on that note...

....

Irony? There's a paper in Britain called
The Sun.

....

I answered the phone. I said 'who's
speaking?' They said 'You are'.

....

They say one in every seven friends have
a gambling addiction.
My money's on Dave.

....

Ladies call me 'The Macarena' because
everyone is trying to forget the time they
did me.

....

I love the woman. I know I love her
because she told me.

....

For an 'adult' bookstore, this place has
a LOT of picture books.

....

We went horse riding and she got her foot caught in the stirrup and she panics. Finished up the manager of the Woolworths had to come out and unplug the horse.

....

In my family I was the youngest of three. My parents were both older.

....

My doctor stutters so I'm not sure if I have pneumonia or double pneumonia.

....

I saw the first James Bond movie where he only has his learner's permit to kill.

....

You know you're from Sydney if you spent more money on your coffee machine than on your washing machine.

....

I went out with a girl until we went shopping for a dress. It was terrible. Fifteen shops, sixty dresses. She was finally like, 'For God's sake. None of them look good on you. Choose one, you weirdo.'

....

What is the deal with bank staff?
What is the busiest time of the banking
day for customers? It's lunchtime and
you've got two windows open. Where
are all the tellers? 'Oh they're at lunch?'
So are we. We choose to come to the bank
instead of having our lunch and we don't
even work here! That doesn't happen
anywhere else. You don't walk into a
restaurant at lunchtime. 'I'm sorry there's
going to be a bit of a wait for the food.
The chefs are all at lunch.'

....

Research has shown that men think
about sex every 15 sex.

....

The side effects of my prescription
are written on the bottle. My medicine
'May cause vomiting, dizziness and
chest pains. If this becomes bothersome
contact your doctor'. How can it be
bothersome?

I like when I'm dizzy. It distracts me
from the fact that I'm vomiting and having
chest pains.

....

As a kid I remember lying in bed at night, looking up at the stars thinking, 'Where the hell is the roof?'

....

I'm reading the Incomplete Works of William Shakespeare. I'm halfway through Romeo and What's-Her-Name.

....

We were at a movie and they made an announcement: 'It's now time to turn your phones to silent. Unless you're with Optus in which case that'd be redundant.'

....

I've discovered that when you dig up dead people here it's a crime. But when you do it in another country it's called archaeology.

....

The only way I can spend time with a girl is to stalk them. But I hate being a stalker. Just once it'd be nice to do what I wanted to do. Stalking can get boring. Here's a tip. Try and stalk someone who's already stalking someone else. And they might be stalking someone else too. One time I was lucky enough to be tenth in a stalking chain. We had our own minibus.

....

About to watch that superhero movie, *The Green Arrow*. I bet his superpower is being able to turn at red lights.

....

I never really knew my mother. She left before I was born.

....

I remember my English teacher asking me to do a book report on a book I hadn't read so I started making it up. I was even using fake words. The teacher said 'What the hell are you talking about?' I said 'I dunno. Can I buy a vowel?' She said, 'You should buy a thesaurus.' I said, 'They're extinct.'

....

Being an actor is tough but I'm in a good mood. I got a very good review this morning. 'Prompt and efficient payer.' — eBay.

....

I knew I was in no condition to drive. But then I thought, 'Wait! I shouldn't listen to myself, I'm drunk!'

....

If I was stuck on a desert island with only one record, I'd want it to be the record for being able to swim the farthest.

....

A bloke wakes up in an army hospital. 'Doc I can't feel my legs!' 'I know. I've amputated your arms.'

....

Ironically, my only steady girlfriend was also the most unstable.

....

I'm not looking forward to the day my dog finds out she's adopted.

....

My wife thinks shorts that show the bottom roundy part of your butt cheek are slutty but I think they're sexy so to hell with her, I'm wearing 'em.

....

I went into a country supermarket. There were two aisles of groceries and eight aisles of salt.

I said to the owner, 'You must sell a lot of salt.' He said, 'No, hardly any actually. But the guy who sells me salt, that guy knows how to sell salt.'

....

I don't like basketball. The shorts are too long, the game is too long and the players are too long.

....

My mate was asleep so we shaved his eyebrows off. He was really surprised but you couldn't tell.

....

Why do mountain climbers tie themselves together with rope? To stop the sensible ones from going home.

....

How do you toilet train King Kong? Hit him with a rolled-up newspaper building.

....

The English horn. So named because it is neither English nor a horn. Unlike the French horn, which is German.

....

My ex-wife has lessons with the devil on how to be more evil. I don't know what she charges him...

....

I did a book signing today. Librarians get angry pretty quick.

....

My friend is a blackjack dealer. On his forearm he has a tattoo of an Ace and a Jack. I'm a blackjack player. On my forearm I'm gonna get a tattoo of a ten and a six. And then another ten.

....

When I fly I like to sit in 1C. Because you're the first off the plane and this gives you enormous power. You can lead 250 passengers wherever you want in the airport.

....

So now I'm an author. But I do my book signings at op shops to save people a trip.

....

I went in for that laser eye surgery. Here's something they don't tell you. After the surgery your eyes don't shoot lasers. I felt like an idiot. I'm staring at bread trying to make toast.

....

Terrorism is obviously on everybody's mind. The other day my son says to me, 'Daddy, how come the bad men hate us?' How sad is that? I actually got tears in my eyes — because he's 18. What kind of a moron am I raising?

....

My father-in-law's been having a hard time lately. Keeps on losing his keys. Can't hang on to a set of keys to save his life. And he has tried everything too: little hook next to the door, little bowl next to his bed, keychain makes a noise when you whistle. Nothing worked. So finally, this year for his birthday, the whole family chipped in — and we put him in a home.

....

To people in Melbourne, Darwin is kind of like the attic. You forget it's up there but when you actually go up there you're like, 'Wow, look at all this stuff!'

....

I was going to join the debating team but someone talked me out of it.

....

Do you know what you're supposed to do for a jellyfish sting? Pee on it. I didn't know that. I'll tell you what though, it doesn't work as well on shark bites. The young boy's family were furious.

....

My extra sensitive toothpaste doesn't like it when I use other toothpastes.

....

First night as bouncer I threw out a drunk. I asked another bouncer at the door when I get my break. He said to ask the boss. I said, where is he? He said, 'He's just coming back in.'

....

In Malaysia, I got arrested at the airport trying to smuggle a porcupine in my underpants. It was unpleasant for both of us.

....

I had the most boring office job in the world. I used to clean the windows on envelopes.

....

I'm in court with an English tourist who'd got done for drugs or something. The judge sentenced us to fifty lashes across the back with the cane, but we were allowed to have one thing on our back to protect us. The Englishman said, 'I'm an Englishman. I don't need any protection. I will take my punishment for the Queen and England.' They asked me what I wanted on my back. I said, 'The Englishman.'

....

I remember back at school, one year there was a new Indian kid from Delhi. Nice kid. The teacher asked him what his name was. He said, 'Rammerjan Vankatranjibannerjee.'

The teacher says, 'How do you spell that?'

The kid says, 'My mother helps me.'

....

The copper said to me, 'Are you going to come quietly, or do I have to use earplugs?'

....

My grandmother was a very tough woman. She buried three husbands and two of them were just napping.

....

The triathlon at the Olympics. They have to practice at swimming, running and cycling. Who has that sort of time? These people don't have jobs, or they have jobs that are incredibly difficult to get to.

....

I was a flight attendant on a helicopter. We had six seats. I'd ask a guy if he'd like something to drink. You would? Then we're going to have to land.

....

Have you seen that ad where the guy is clicking his fingers and he says, 'Every time I click my fingers, a child dies'? I watched that, and couldn't help thinking, 'Well stop clicking your fingers!'

....

I rang up Telstra. I said, 'I want to report a nuisance caller.' They said, 'Not you again.'

....

I was hosting an office stationery exhibition. I was talking to a lady. I said, 'You're the woman that invented Liquid Paper, correct me if I'm wrong...'

....

A few years ago, driving through the outback, I found a bloke lying on the road, covered in blood. I said, 'What happened mate?'

He said, 'It was a blue Holden Ute, with three blokes in the front, with a big aerial, NSW plates and thirty cases of beer in the back.'

I said, 'How do you know all that?'

He said, 'I fell out of the thing five minutes ago.'

....

A couple visited the doctor, saying they needed advice on making love so they jump up on his table and get into it. He looks at them and says, 'It looks fine to me.' They're back the next week, wanting more advice and get into it again. They come back the next week and the doctor says, 'You two are absolutely fine. Why do you keep coming in here wanting advice on sex?' The bloke says, 'Alright Doc, I'll level with ya. We can't go to her place because she's married, we can't go to my place because I'm married. A hotel costs two hundred bucks, a motel costs a hundred bucks, you cost fifty and we get half back on Medicare.'

....

A bloke rings 000. 'Send the ambulance.
My wife's having a baby.'

The operator said, 'Is this her first baby?'

He said, 'No it's her husband, Frank.'

....

I went into a hardware shop. I said,
'I want to buy 20,000 bricks for a BBQ.'

The guy said, 'You don't need 20,000 bricks
to make a BBQ.'

I said, 'You do if you live in the 17th floor.'

....

I'm a total prefectionist.

....

If my builder had the job of building Rome:

EMPEROR: How long will it take you to build
Rome?

MY BUILDER: A day.

EMPEROR: Really? Are you sure?

MY BUILDER: Absolutely. Trust me.

....

I've failed more maths exams than
I can count.

....

Just sitting here wondering why things sent by car are called shipments and things sent by ships are called cargo.

....

The last time I was someone's type I was donating blood.

....

Do you think that elevators should have a different name when they're going down?

....

The directions on every jar of anti-aging cream should read: 'Apply liberally to face and neck 20 years ago.'

....

We're starting a sarcasm club. It really would mean the world to me if you joined.
Really.

....

A cop pulled me over on the freeway.
He said, 'Why were you going so fast?'
I said, 'You see this peddle down here?
It's called an accelerator. The more you push it, the faster you go.'
You'd think they'd train these guys.

....

Captain Hook was talking to a bloke in a bar. The bloke said, 'You look like you've lived a tough life. How did you lose your leg?'

Captain Hook said, 'I got in a fight with a crocodile and he bit off my leg so I had to get a peg leg.'

The bloke said, 'How did you get the hook?'

The captain said, 'I was in a sword fight with a guy and he cut off my hand, so I had to get the hook.'

The bloke said, 'And the eye patch?'

Captain Hook said, 'I was down at the beach and it was a beautiful blue sky. I looked up to admire the view and a seagull pooped in my eye.'

The bloke said, 'Are you telling me you lost an eye from poop?'

The captain said, 'No, but I'd only had the hook for two days.'

....

Sitting in bar in Transylvania.

ME: So, Dr. Frankenstein, how do you make a living?

DR. FRANKENSTEIN: How do I make a living what?

....

On a first date:

HER: You haven't removed many bras have you?

ME: What gave it away?

HER: The scissors, mainly.

....

There's nothing horribler than a word that isn't real.

....

'EVERYONE THROW YOUR ARMS UP!!': Food poisoning scare at Cannibal Club.

....

My friend has 6-year-old twin boys and they hate to brush their teeth. So he just convinced them that it's fun to brush someone else's teeth. Problem solved.

....

I kicked him right where the sun don't shine *(Iceland)*.

....

Well-known brands really are better. For instance, I just found out that the Preen pen works much better on stains than a regular pen.

....

I told my wife I was going to fix our clothes dryer myself. She said she was proud of me and while I was doing that she was going to Harvey Norman to choose our new clothes dryer.

....

A bloke from Brisbane needed work so he went to the outback and applied for a job at the mines. The foreman asked him if he had any experience, because they only hired people with experience. The Brisbane bloke said, 'Absolutely. I've worked on oil rigs, gas, copper mines and coal.'

'Really?' said the foreman. 'That's impressive. How deep underground have you been on the coal mines?'

The bloke said 'Ten miles down.'

'Ten miles?!!' said the foreman, starting to get suspicious.

So he decided to ask the bloke a trick question. 'That's pretty deep. What kind of lighting did they use down that deep?'

The bloke said, 'I don't know, I was on the day shift.'

....

'I'm completely over my ex', is the name of my poem to her.

....

I don't know how Halloween's Michael Myers put up with all that screaming. It'd drive me crazy.

....

Yes your honour, I did it. But in my defence, I thought she'd been stung by a jellyfish.

....

Naming that movie that's set in space 'Gravity' makes as much sense as naming the movie 'Arachnophobia' something like 'No Spiders'.

....

Twitter may be turning 14 years old, but it still reads and writes at a 6-year-old level.

....

You stereotypes are all the same.

....

Pavlov walks into a bar. The phone rings and he says, 'Damn, I forgot to feed the dog.'

....

A bloke was riding a horse through the outback when the horse decided that it wasn't going to run any more. No matter what the bloke did, he couldn't get the horse to go any quicker than a slow walk. As it turned out he was on the outskirts of a small town. He walked the horse up the main street and saw a sign that said 'horse garage'. He took the horse in and the mechanic said 'What's up?'

The bloke said, 'I can't get this bloody horse to run.' The mechanic said, 'Put him up on the hoist and I'll sort it out.'

So the bloke lead the horse onto the hoist, the mechanic raised the hoist up and then grabbed two bricks and went underneath the horse and smacked them together on the horse's private parts. The horse let out a squawk and bolted out of the garage and ran down the street at a hundred miles an hour. The bloke turned to the mechanic and said, 'Well that's fantastic but how am I supposed to catch him now?'

The mechanic said, 'No worries. Get up on the hoist.'

Dear diary, sometimes it seems like I can't tell if something is an inanimate object or a real person.

PSYCHIATRIST: 'So I see.'

....

I stopped understanding maths when the alphabet decided to get involved.

....

Alcohol won't solve your problems, but it can give you an interesting set of new ones.

....

My friend from Limbo club and I go way back.

....

Why don't you ever see elephants hiding in trees? Because they're really good at it.

....

I think there are times when tattoo artists need to take control and say, 'No, I'm not doing that.'

....

I've got this great idea for a future failed business.

....

ME: I love you and I will always keep
you safe.

DAUGHTER: What about spiders?

ME: I love you and I will sometimes
keep you safe.

....

So I'm doing the crossword with the dog
at my feet.

ME: OK, pup star, I need help. 'Outer
coating of tree. Four letters.'

DOG: Woof?

ME: Bad dog!

....

Listen up, cooking directions on the sides
of packages: Nobody knows the wattage
of their microwave!

....

Every time you spell it 'tho,' I say 'ugh,'
so it ends up being spelled right.

....

I think a wasp's nest chucked through the
window would be the ideal way to end any
hostage situation.

....

I'm going to learn sign language because it's handy.

....

I'm confused because I read that the right side of the brain controls the left side of the body, meaning leftists are the only ones in their right mind.

....

I opened my electric bill and my water bill at the same time.

I was shocked.

....

Boxing and Fencing are similar in that they both have nothing to do with boxes and fences.

....

What do you call someone who points out the obvious?

Someone who points out the obvious.

....

Everyone I've ever met has told me to stop exaggerating.

....

After losing a bet I had to go into town wearing a miniskirt and no undies which showed a lot of balls.

....

MEDICAL RECEPTIONIST: 'So you're here about your carpal tunnel wrist? Fine. Please fill out these 20 forms and press hard so the copies are clear.'

....

Cinderella is my favourite story about choosing a spouse based on shoe size.

....

Knocking a full drink over in a bar as an adult is the equivalent of letting go of a helium balloon as a child.

....

Pretty sure the voice of reason is hoarse by now. 'Aw, to hell with you.'

....

I just saw an Apple store getting robbed.

Police want to talk to me because I'm an iWitness.

....

I really hope phone inventor Alexander Graham Bell's nickname was Lord Of The Rings.

....

We're using all the stuff in our fridge that's about to go out of date. So tonight, we're having buttered olives with mustard and baking soda.

....

They say there's a person capable of murder in every group of friends. I suspected it was Dan, so I killed him before he could do something silly.

....

I've never used the phrase 'cul de sac' in a sentence.

Well, until now, anyway.

....

I always keep a shotgun under my bed in case a horse sneaks in and breaks his leg.

....

78% of pie-eating contests take place alone in a kitchen at midnight.

....

GYM INSTRUCTOR: '...and over here are the free weights.'

ME: *(shoving weights in my pockets)* 'Fantastic.'

....

I hope when I inevitably choke to death on gummy bears people just say I was killed by bears and leave it at that.

....

I have a rule in legal matters: I refuse to sign anything unless they give me time to pretend to read it first.

....

Proud to say I did my first book signing today. I wrote my name in 27 books before the librarian threw me out.

....

Sex education classes in school should just be listening to a baby crying for six straight hours while watching the same episode of *Peppa Pig* on repeat.

....

The Incredible Hulk has died.
RIP

....

I'm in hospital because I ate what I thought was an onion, but it was a daffodil bulb.

It's OK though. The doctors reckon I'll be out in the Spring.

....

The natives gathered around my lighter in awe, for they were smokers, and had misplaced their matches.

....

Bad ways to meet people #14:

'Hi, I'm Marty.'

'Yes, we've met.'

(Trying to save face)
'Really? When was that?'

'Twenty minutes ago.'

....

I went to the barbers.

I said, 'How much for a haircut?'

He said, '$50.'

I said, 'How much for a shave?'

He said, '$20.'

I said, 'OK, shave my head.'

....

They've just had a study that tried to pinpoint the effect that alcohol has on walking.

The result was staggering.

....

My first girlfriend left me because she said I was obsessed with the Muppets.

Apparently I wasn't ready for a kermitment.

....

Congrats once again to 'Shiny, Swaying Thing' for sweeping the Feline Choice Awards.

....

If I could choose one super power right now it would be the ability to delete my number from other people's phones.

....

We're having a recycling party tonight at my place. Bring a bottle. And some cans and cardboard.

....

I have two kids. One's gonna be a lawyer and one's gonna need a lawyer.

....

My uncle got arrested for theft but said he was innocent so he took a lie detector test. And got $50 for it at Cash Converters.

....

Coyotes are dangerous so stay away. This advice will lessen your chances of being hit by an anvil.

....

A bloke from the city decided to go to an outback country race meeting. About halfway through the day he needed to go to the toilet. When he went in he noticed that everyone was doing their business into a big deep trench full of all sorts of muck as you can imagine. Another man came in stood beside him and as the man was having a wee, he pulled his handkerchief out and a 20-cent coin came out of his pocket and dropped into the pit. He watched it sink into the crap then pulled a $50 bill out of his pocket and threw it in the pit as well.

The city bloke said, 'What the hell did you do that for?'

The man said, 'You don't think I was going to dive into that muck for 20 cents do you?'

....

They've got a cure for the fear of flying.
22 hours on a bus.

....

Bob Marley must be rolling in his grave.

....

Crocodiles are faster than humans on
land and water which means if you're up
against one in a triathlon, you'd better
nail the bike leg.

....

I'm no 'Tour de France' expert but it
seems that the best way to win is to wear
a yellow shirt.

....

If God had a sense of humour he would
have asked Noah to bring a pair of
termites on board.

....

Boxing. 'And in the red corner, the
undisputed champion of the world!'
If it's undisputed, what's all the
fighting about?

....

I love the dirty look people give the footpath when they turn around after they trip on it.

....

I think Sony, Hitachi and Pioneer are just stereotypes.

....

He jumps out of the plane and begins reading the parachute instruction manual.

STEP 1: PUT ON PARACHUTE.

He looks up.

'Damn...'

....

When I'm walking down the street and someone walks next to me at the same speed I want to grab their hand and start skipping.

....

The guy who invented Tetris died.
At his burial, as soon as the coffin fitted in the grave an entire line of mourners disappeared.

....

My new issue of Kidnapper's Weekly makes cutting out letters for ransom notes a breeze!

....

'Hurry', she said. 'Stand in the corner.'

She rubbed baby oil all over him then dusted him with talcum powder. 'Don't move until I tell you. Pretend you're a statue.'

'What's this?' the husband said as he entered the room.

'Oh it's a statue,' she replied. 'The Smiths bought one and I liked it so I got one for us, too.'

No more was said, not even when they went to bed.

Around 2 AM the husband got up, went to the kitchen and returned with a sandwich and a beer.

'Here,' he said to the statue, 'Have this. I stood like that for two days at the Smiths and nobody offered me a damned thing.'

....

FOR SALE: Used Tombstone. Would really suit someone named Frank Johnston.

....

I had to use my Coles discount card to scrape bird poo from my windscreen. Didn't work though. I only got 10% off.

....

My friend died because we didn't know his blood type. As he was slipping away he said 'Be positive', but I know he was just being brave.

....

FOR SALE: Trailer. No wheels. To collect you'll need a trailer.

....

I got robbed at a service station. I called the cops and when they arrived they asked if I knew who did it? I said 'It was pump number 7.'

....

I'm going to get a front door mat that says 'Just text me'.

....

I rented a tuxedo then didn't need it. Do you know how hard it is to sublet a tuxedo?

....

'Easy Come, Easy Go' is the best name ever for a prostate clinic.

....

Are you looking for a safe job? Well we're doing one Friday night. Contact Little Jimmy or Cracker McGee.

....

A bloke decided to buy a cattle station. About a year later his mate came out to visit him from the city. He said, 'What did you finish up calling the station?'

The bloke said, 'The Lazy T Bar Triple Seven Rocking Diamond Wandering Bronco Ranch.'

His mate said, 'That's quite a name. How come I don't see any cattle?'

The bloke said 'None of them survived the branding.'

....

FOR SALE: Miniature poodle. Large.

....

This looks like a job for
   (I rip open my jacket)
Jacket Repair Man!
   (I sew my jacket back together)

....

I'm sure that 90% of the software on my computer doesn't do anything except send me notifications that there's a new version of itself.

....

I've found people's insecurities about their bodies are a bigger turnoff than their body ever could be.

....

I'm starting to feel like I'm only around to drive the plot forward in someone else's life.

....

My wife just left me because of my obsession with cricket.

It's really hit me for 6.

....

FOR SALE: Human Skull. Used.

....

My tummy just made a really strange noise. So I'm just going to send a BBQ chicken and some potato salad down to check it out.

....

'The problem with quotes on the internet is that you can never tell if they're genuine.'

– Albert Einstein.

....

To punish my daughter I don't take away her phone, I take away her charger and then I watch her terror as her battery dies. Good times.

....

Dis earing letters?

There's an 'app' for that.

....

ME: I know I can't get this star on top of the Christmas tree without it all falling over and smashing the glass coffee table.

BOURBON: Yes you can.

....

At the cafe today they had a jar beside the register that said 'tip jar' so I did and all the coins fell out.

....

How long does it take for an avocado to brown after you cut it... never mind.

....

'Hello you've reached my voicemail. Please leave your name, number and a damn good reason why you couldn't just text me.'

A bloke suspected his wife was having an affair. So one day he came home from work early and rushed upstairs to find her lying in bed, alone. He turned and looked out the window and saw a man running along the street putting a shirt on. He was furious, and in a blind rage, picked up a fridge and threw it out the window at the man. Then he had a heart attack from the strain and died.

The next thing he knew, he was at the Pearly Gates in heaven. He told Saint Peter what had happened and went inside. The next guy in the queue stepped up and Saint Peter asked him what had happened to him. He said, 'I was running late for an appointment and took a shortcut up a side street and someone dropped a fridge on me.' He went into heaven. Then the next guy in the queue stepped up and said, 'Well I was hiding in this fridge...'

I would never cheat in a relationship. Because that would require two people finding me attractive.

....

My corduroy pillow has been making headlines all week.

....

HER: I'm worried the romance has gone out of our marriage.

ME: I bet I can change your mind during the next commercial break.

....

I used to like tractors but I don't anymore.

I guess you could call me an extractor fan.

....

What do you call two blokes sitting on top of a window?

Kurt and Rod.

....

I learnt something today. Don't fart in an Apple store.

They don't have Windows.

....

A guy got a job at Melbourne Zoo and was put in charge of the exotic animals exhibit. His boss told him that he needed to get some interesting animals from around the world to add to the zoo's collection. So he wrote a letter to Capetown Zoo in South Africa.

> 'Dear Sirs.
> I work at Melbourne zoo. I'd like you to send me two mongooses.'

But that didn't look right, so he crossed out 'mongooses' and wrote 'mongeese'. But that didn't look right either so he started again.

> 'Dear Sirs.
> I work at Melbourne zoo and I'd like you to send me a mongoose. Actually while you're at it, send me another one too.'

....

I did a First Aid Course. The instructor asks me, 'What would you do if your child swallowed the front door key?'

I said, 'Climb through the window.'

....

I've just invented a new flavour of potato chip. If they go well I'll make a packet.

....

'People who quote themselves are idiots.'
  – *Marty Fields.*

....

My wife always accuses me of having a favourite child. It's not true, I love Hayley and Not-Hayley equally.

....

My doctor has diagnosed me with '70s Fever'.
It flares up occasionally.

....

Yawning is your body's way of saying 20% battery remaining.

....

A new study has shown that people will believe anything as long as you start by saying, 'A new study has shown...'

....

I was driving on the freeway in a hearse. Police pulled me over for undertaking.

....

My mate said, 'It's me and my wife's
ten-year anniversary next weekend.
I thought we could go somewhere really
nice together.'

I said 'Sounds good to me, mate.
But what are you going to tell your wife?'

....

When I was a kid I was kidnapped. I was
surprised to find that despite the name,
there is no napping involved. I was
awake the whole time which made it
all pretty tiring.

....

My friend told me an onion is the only food
that can make you cry, so I threw a coconut
at his face.

....

Diets are easy. I don't mean to brag but
I just finished a 14-day diet in two and a
half hours.

....

Girls, you know your boyfriend's getting fat
when he fits into your husband's clothes.

....

I rarely swim because it's rarely more than 30 minutes since I last ate.

....

My wife says I plan too far ahead.
Our first date hasn't started too well.

....

Just woke up to find a spoon in my mouth, a tea bag in my left eye and milk in my right eye. I'm sick of my mates treating me like a mug.

....

The problem with the campaign to decriminalise marijuana is people keep losing the petitions.

....

I'm at a job interview and the guy says, 'It says here your interests include connecting people.'

I said, 'Actually that's "correcting" people.'

....

Last night I did my joke about Peter Pan again.

Never gets old.

....

Dressing as the Grim Reaper for my first day at my new job didn't get the laughs I thought it would. People in casualty are so uptight.

....

I took my car to the mechanic today because it was making a terrible noise. Turned out it was just my daughter's music playlist.

....

Which spice girl can hold the most petrol? Geri can.

....

I'm pretty annoyed. Every morning a huge German Shepherd poos on my front lawn.

And to make matters worse, today he brought his dog.

....

I, for one, like Roman numerals.

....

My daughter wanted a train set for Christmas but I can't find a good one so I'm getting her a replacement bus service.

....

Hippopotamuses kill more people every year than guns which surprises me because guns are easier to hide on you. You have the element of surprise. Nobody has ever been arrested for carrying a concealed hippopotamus.

....

'Be proud of every single idea you come up with.'

– *Anonymous.*

....

I met my first girlfriend on a blind date. She was standing in the middle of a tennis court. I said, 'You must be Annette.'

....

A lot of people that appear 'cool' actually struggle with feelings of inadequacy.

Not me. I have those feelings without appearing cool at all.

....

My wife isn't talking to me because apparently I ruined her birthday. I'm not sure how I did that. I didn't even know it WAS her birthday.

....

I've just sold my homing pigeons on eBay for the 17th time.

....

I said to my Doctor, 'You've got to help me, I'm addicted to Twitter!' He said 'I don't follow you.'

....

You're in bed. Your alarm goes off at 6.30, you close your eyes for 5 minutes and it's 8:45.

You're at work. It's 14:30. You close your eyes for 5 minutes and it's 14:29.

....

It's good to see that reincarnation is making a comeback.

....

I bet that iceberg was surprised when it was hit by the Titanic because 85% of a ship is hidden above the surface.

....

I've written a book about Australia's finest basements.

It's already on the best cellars list.

....

I can see twelve months into the future.
I must have 2020 vision.

....

Comas can really change the meaning
of a sentence.

For example:

'Ben is in a hurry.'

'Ben is in a coma.'

....

You know you're a bad driver when your
Sat Nav says 'In 300 metres, stop and let
me out'.

....

I've learnt you can only say 'Look at you!
You got so big!' to children.

Adults tend to get offended.

....

I saw a guy in the library reading a book
at least two feet thick.

I asked him why he was reading such
a huge book.

He said, 'It's a long story.'

....

Maybe eating that pie was not cheating on this diet. Maybe going on this diet was cheating on that pie.

....

My next-door neighbour works as a psychic. One time I had a suit that was too big for me so I offered it to him but he said it wouldn't fit him either. He's a medium.

....

I organised a surprise party for my wife. I led her into the living room wearing a blindfold. As I tripped over a chair she said, 'Um, shouldn't I be wearing that?'

....

If, like me, you struggle to open a bottle of champagne, hit it with a ship. That works well.

....

'For the last time, do not leave your gold and diamonds lying around the mansion!'
– *My plumber to his kids.*

....

Drugs and alcohol are never the answer. Unless someone asks me, 'What are you doing next weekend?'

....

My friend named his son Oscar just so at the birth the obstetrician had to say 'And the Oscar goes to...'

....

I was having a dip at the swimming pool when the lifeguard asked, 'What have you got there?' I said, 'Tzatziki'.

....

Last night I got stopped by a cop using a radar gun. He starts asking me all sorts of questions like where I'd got the radar gun.

....

I spent all day yesterday floating out in the bay.

It's been my dream ever since I was a little buoy.

....

I just took some sleeping pills for my insomnia but they don't seem to be wor

....

My uncle died of a heart attack on the golf course. My auntie said 'At least he died doing what he loved.' That's stupid. Who loves having a heart attack?

....

My wife told me she thought we'd have less arguments if I wasn't so pedantic.

I said, 'I think you mean fewer.'

....

All those years of getting horrible primary school pictures was just society's way of preparing you for your driver's license photo.

....

I don't need glasses. I'm in my fifties. I know where everything is.

....

I said to a mate, 'What's your pet hate?'

He said, 'He doesn't like it when the vet puts a thermometer up his bum.'

....

Comedy was tough at first. There was no money in it. Have you ever asked a dentist 'How much for cash?'

....

DOCTOR: Are you allergic to anything?

ME: Cats.

DOCTOR: Anything else?

ME: Grease.

DOCTOR: Any other musicals?

The inventor of the hard drive has died. Thanks for the memory.

I'll bet the first ever McDonalds drive thru window resulted in an incredible amount of broken glass.

There's eight *Fast and the Furious* movies and not once, in any of them, have they stopped for petrol.

Yesterday I met a client for 'Brunch' which I thought was a cross between lunch and break dancing. It didn't go well.

Raising children takes a village, preferably one with a brewery.

My dad always said 'Don't believe everything you hear.'

It was great advice.

Or was it?

....

The difference between running and jogging is that runners compete in races and joggers find dead bodies on *Law and Order.*

....

West End beer doesn't give you a hangover.

Nobody can drink enough of that crap to get one.

....

I remember when my 13-year-old daughter was four years old and dropped glitter on the couch. It came to mind today as I continue to clean that glitter off the couch.

....

(Enter Password)

handbag

(Re-enter Password)

shoes

(Error: Passwords must match)

....

In Bermuda it will cost you $4.00 for a steak pie, and in Jamaica it will cost you $5.00.

These are pie rates of the Caribbean.

....

I remember getting kicked out of class at school and the teacher yelling at me, 'What would your parents say if I called them?'

I said, 'Hello?'

....

I wish I could remember the name of that big bird in *Sesame Street*.

....

My parents were always pestering me to have kids. They'd say, 'Who will carry on the ancient family curse?'

....

Welcome to Hypochondriac Club.
Uh oh, Jim looks a bit pale. Jim you shouldn't have come if you're sick.
Now I feel pale. Do I look pale...?

....

I asked my wife 'What do you want me to do with this big roll of bubble wrap?'

She said, 'Just pop it in the corner.'

It took me four hours.

....

With all those missiles getting launched I'm starting to think North Korea just really hates the ocean.

....

Apparently there's a nudist convention on in town next week. I might go if I've got nothing on.

....

When I worked at McDonalds I wanted to specialise in making ice creams so they sent me to sundae school.

....

'Get Well Soon' is a great thing to write on a card for someone whose home's had their water supply cut off.

....

Not sure if you'll like golf? Walk on a treadmill for four hours under a sun lamp then throw away $75 when you're finished.

....

At the park there's a sign that says
'No dogs' and I'm there with my two dogs.
Some guy says, 'The sign says no dogs.'
I said, 'Then the sign's wrong.'

....

Just how hairy was the person
who invented a shampoo called
Head & Shoulders?

....

I took my mate's twins to a maze and
started them at two different points so
people thought they kept passing the
same kid. Confusion is easy to create.

....

The health food shop just notified me
that somehow I've won a 'Lifetime
Supply of Fresh Kale' which in my case
is one kale.

....

(At a funeral)

ME: 'Do you mind if I say a word?'

WIDOW: 'Please do.'

(I go to the lectern)

ME: 'Plethora!'

WIDOW: 'Thank you. That means a lot.'

....

Twenty-four movies and so far nobody has ever called James Bond 'Jimmy'.

....

Three reasons why men are lazy.

1) Because we're men.

2) Because

3)

....

I can't get my joke about long-term unemployed people to work.

....

My personal computer just crashed now all our other computers have slowed down to have a look.

....

MAN WITH A BEARD 50 YEARS AGO:
'Going to the forest to chop down trees.'

MAN WITH A BEARD TODAY: 'Going to the shop, there's a new gluten-free body scrub.'

....

I saved a heap of money on my car insurance simply by not pulling over after I hit that guy.

....

I just got a speed camera photo in the mail. I sent it back. Way too expensive and really bad quality.

....

There are eleven types of people in the world: those that understand Roman numerals, and those that don't.

....

I heard someone got sick in a restaurant from eating a meal that wasn't properly Instagrammed.

....

Every boy band song should have a part where they realise they're singing about the same girl and get mad at each other.

....

Long distance relationships are too hard. Refrigerator, you're coming to the bedroom.

....

A pterodactyl walks into a bar and says, 'Ptequila, pthanks.'

....

Don't call me a party animal then get upset when I poo on your carpet.

....

They say 'Give a man a fish and he'll eat for a day'. To be honest, if some random dude just walked up and gave me a fish, I'd be unlikely to eat it.

....

Yesterday we were on a mystery coach tour so we had a sweepstakes to guess where we were going. The driver won fifty bucks.

....

What a day. My pet snake dictated a letter to me so I was just sitting at the computer for him hitting the 's' key.

....

'KIDS, GET YOUR SHOES ON. WE'RE LEAVING FOR SCHOOL IN SIX HOURS!!'

– Centipede parents.

....

At a spelling bee:

JUDGE: Your word is 'asterisk'.

KID: Can you use it in a sentence?

JUDGE: You've won a car. *conditions apply

....

Apparently over a quarter of pet owners let their pets sleep on the bed with them. I tried it, but my goldfish died.

....

'First time flying huh?'

'Yeah how could you tell?'

'Just a hunch. The overhead bin is usually for luggage. You wanna come down to your seat?'

....

When my doctor told me my rash wasn't contagious I wasn't convinced. It was the way he shouted it across the car park.

....

My budgie broke his leg so I made him a tiny splint out of a couple of matches. His little face lit up when he tried to walk.

....

(mailman delivers package to hospital)

NURSE: Ah, this is just what the
doctor ordered!

MAILMAN: Do you have to do that every time?

....

People who tell boastful lies on Twitter and
Facebook make me laugh till my chiselled
abs hurt.

....

The first rule of elevator club is don't make
eye contact or talk to other members of
elevator club.

....

SHOPPING WITH A FRIEND: 'Look, triangle-
shaped Tupperware for your
leftover pizza!'

ME: 'What's leftover pizza?

....

Frankly, auto correct, I'm getting tired
of your shirt.

....

I think my main problem is that I have
really fantastic bad ideas.

....

I applied for a government job but accidentally sent the wrong resume. This early display of incompetence should work in my favour.

....

If you're looking for quality, never buy fireworks from a guy with more than seven fingers.

....

I think my main problem is that I have really fantastic bad ideas.

....

I imagine a handshake means something completely different to a cannibal.

....

People who sometimes use the wrong words should have the humidity to admit it.

....

I'm pretty sure I'll die trying to pat something I shouldn't.

....

If I owned a copying shop I'd hire identical twins to work in it.

....

This weight loss website wants me to accept cookies. Hmm...

....

I can't believe how long I've been reading this motivational book called 'Task Completion'.

....

I asked my wife if I could just have a little peace and quiet while I cooked dinner. So she took the battery out of the smoke detector.

....

My favourite part of clothes shopping is going into fitting rooms, waiting 5 minutes then yelling, 'Hey! There's no toilet paper in here!'

....

'I'm not a big dog person.'
    – *A werewolf lying to you.*

....

My optometry jokes are getting cornea and cornea.

....

Shhh!

Shhh!

Shhh!

Shhh!

Shhh!

Shhh!

Shhh!

Shhh!

Shhh!

Shhh!

Shhh!

– *Librarians arguing.*

....

How about an air horn that looks like a can of air freshener so you will always know when a visitor poos at your house.

....

(As I pull back your shower curtain)
'What did you mean by "creepy"?'

....

Our vet is great. If you take your dog in and you have pet insurance, they give you a courtesy dog for the day.

....

At the physio clinic I parked in the staff car park. An attendant came up and said, 'This is for badge holders only'.

I said, 'I know. I've got a bad shoulder.'

....

Scared the postman today by going to the door naked.

I'm not sure what scared him more, my naked body or the fact that I knew where he lived.

....

I've just finished reading a book called *How To Give Constructive Criticism*.

It was rubbish.

....

SHEEPDOG: All 50 sheep are accounted for.

FARMER: But I only had 49?

SHEEPDOG: Yeah I know. I rounded them up.

....

The Grim Reaper came for me last night but I managed to fight him off with a vacuum cleaner. Talk about Dyson with death.

....

My WiFi has stopped working. Turns out our neighbours hadn't paid the bill.

....

I take a cup out of the dishwasher but I don't know where it goes so I put it on the sink. My wife sees it and puts it in the dishwasher. This has been going on for 18 months.

....

I tried to read a book called *The History of Sellotape* but I couldn't find the beginning.

....

I'm surprised I haven't heard from my doctor since my ear surgery.

Wait...

....

I lost my licence so I bought a vintage Rolls Royce because I thought it came with a driver. It didn't. So I spent all that money and I've got nothing to chauffeur it.

....

All the Scrabble games in our house end with us throwing Scrabble tiles at each other. It's all fun and games until someone loses an i.

....

FOR SALE: Limited Edition bottle of Liquid Paper.

It's a corrector's item.

....

Yesterday was the first day of spring and the first day of my diet so I removed all the bad food from our house.

It was delicious.

....

I think abs are for guys that don't have the confidence to wear a nice T-shirt to the pool.

....

I bet a lot of Smurfs have died because nobody realised they were choking.

....

I don't mean to brag, but I'm in my 50s but my bank account makes me look like I'm 19.

....

My parents admitted that the night I was conceived they'd shared about a dozen beers.

Not easy finding out you're a Fosters child.

....

When I was a kid in trouble at school
my family moved to another area hoping it'd
help the situation. It didn't. I found them.

....

I said to the guy at Baker's Delight,
'How come all your cakes are $2 but
that one's $4?'
He said, 'That's Madeira cake.'

....

TEXT:

WIFE: Love you babe xxx

ME: Love you too

WIFE: It'd mean a lot if you started putting
x's at the end of your texts

ME: OK. Lisa, Danni, Belinda...

....

Times New Roman walks into a bar.
The barman says 'Get out of here!
We don't serve your type.'

....

Whose idea was it to pack a new pair
of scissors in a package that requires
scissors to open it?

....

Can we have a war on beer?

....

As I sit on the plane, I want to say 'How about putting that screaming kid on vibrate?'

....

My sister-in-law won a lifetime supply of chocolate. When the first lot of it arrived she ate 12 kilos of it in one afternoon and died. So they were right.

....

I'm glad I'm learning how to break wooden boards in karate class in case I ever get in a fight with a house.

....

Rick Astley will lend you any of the Pixar films in his collection, except one.

He's never gonna give you Up.

....

I just ordered an iPhone 7 and Apple emailed me to let me know I've already lost the ear buds.

....

ME: Play Mario Brothers with me. I played it as a kid. It's from back when video games made sense.

KID: Why did he jump on a turtle?

ME: Because he's a plumber.

....

I told my wife I wanted an anniversary gift that'd take my breath away. She got me a treadmill.

....

'Gymnasium' in Ancient Greek means 'Naked Excercise' but try telling that to the gym security.

....

KID: We're playing Star Wars. I'm Princess Leia and mum is Luke Skywalker.

ME: What am I?

KID: In the way.

....

There was a problem this morning when I backed the car out of our driveway. The problem was that last night I'd backed it in.

....

My mate tipped me a horse at 25-1 and told me to have my shirt on it. It came first and I won 25 shirts.

....

Whenever I travel I always fly in business class. At least till they send me back to my own seat.

....

My wife told me I suffer from a lack of imagination. I said 'Oh yeah? Well you suffer from a lack of imagination.'

....

I don't get why gyms have so many mirrors. I know what I look like. That's why I'm there.

....

I called triple 0 emergency and I was on hold for ten minutes! When they finally answered I said, 'You're lucky this is a hoax'.

....

The funeral for the man who invented Chinese whispers will be held on Monday. Pass it on.

....

I was a fat kid. When I was born there were stretch marks on my dad.

....

I saw on the news that a student died, two weeks after falling from a balcony in Sydney. I'm thinking, 'Wow, how high was that balcony?'

....

I just ended a long-term relationship.

It wasn't mine, but...

....

How did factory outlet malls get popular? They sell mistakes. I saw a pair of pants with a collar. We nearly bought a grandmother clock.

....

I ordered a home weightlifting set. They're sending me one piece a week. It's done nothing for me but the postman's absolutely buffed.

....

We used to have four different remote controls then we bought a Universal Remote. Now we have five different remote controls.

....

Our pet bird dived into his water bowl
but it was way too shallow. Now he's
a parrotplegic.

....

My wife and I spent our first date sitting in
front of the fire. It was very romantic until
the fire trucks turned up.

....

A girl came up to me after the show last
night and asked if she could have my
number. I told her to get her own number.

....

I do all my own stunts.

Just not on purpose.

....

I called the vet to complain about a bill.
He just put the phone down. As quickly and
humanely as possible.

....

I never feel better about myself than
when I'm doing the Lord's work;
judging people.

....

You can tell whether my last turn was a right or a left by where in my backseat all of the half-empty water bottles are.

....

'You've reached the incontinence hotline. Can you hold please?'

....

'I don't care where we eat' actually means 'Let's have a huge fight and end up eating toasted sandwiches over the sink'.

....

Teenage girls: 'Talk to the scalp 'cause the face ain't lookin' up from my phone.'

....

Where on my donor card do I indicate that my organs are not to be used to save anyone who pronounces it 'eck-cetera?'

....

'It's over there near Bunnings'

    – directions to anywhere.

....

Keith Richards maintains his body by spending a minimum of three hours each day on a hot dog roller.

....

'This is a hallway so if we want to stand around and talk we should move off to the side so people can easily get through.'

— *Nobody.*

....

Matt Preston looks like he folds out into a bed.

....

If you've been married for more than five years and your spouse is in shape they're cheating on you.

....

The hardest part of being a parent is pretending that throwing stuff into a running ceiling fan isn't the most awesome thing ever.

....

A ferret owner's house is the only man-made structure that can be smelled from space.

....

If you pronounce the 'g' in 'fishing' you've never been.

....

'Hi, I'm Margaret, but most people call me Peg.'

'Why?'

'I've never known.'

....

They say you should never go to bed angry so my wife and I decided to stay up and talk about it and now we're going to bed furious.

....

I just ate some really good expensive cheese or some really rotten cheap cheese.

....

My autobiography will be called 'Actually, cashews are legumes, not nuts' and Other Reasons I'm not Invited to Parties.

....

If you took all of the George Foreman grills ever sold and laid them end to end, at least they'd be getting used for something.

....

That which doesn't kill me is everything so far.

....

Today's hairstyle is called, 'And I didn't brush my teeth either'.

....

I've already gained back ten of the five kilos I lost last summer.

....

If we go out to eat and you keep trying to talk to me after the food arrives I'll call the cops.

....

My daughter eats pizza upside-down so I asked her why and she said it was so the yummy part was on her tongue and where's her Nobel prize?

....

How many GWS fans does it take to change a lightbulb?

Both of them.

....

My wife is out of town and I'm a little lonely so tonight I'm going to pay a hooker to come over and fall asleep on my couch at 9:00.

....

In hell all the corn chips are slightly wider than the opening on the salsa jar.

....

When I dance I look like I'm carrying a boiling hot pot of soup with my bare hands and can't find a place to put it down.

....

I put the 'redundancy' in 'redundancy'.

....

I'm caught in a love heptadecagon with the other 16 members of my maths club.

....

Hey SUVs with a spare tyre on the back – we get it, you own an extra tyre, you show offs.

....

Long term relationships are watching someone you love slowly disintegrate. But perhaps I'm romanticising it.

....

If the vans a-rockin', I'm trying to take my coat off without unbuckling my seat belt.

....

I looked over the fence and saw my neighbour having sex with his banana lounge.

He treats objects like women.

....

It's almost impossible to find a Hallmark card to say 'Sorry I missed your birthday then wrecked your mum's Kia with a stolen forklift'.

....

I've done my best to teach my kid about racism, but she's still against it.

....

Any horse can be a seahorse if he's lost enough.

....

I sincerely regret every nap I passed up on as a child.

....

I want to meet the idiot that named them diet pills instead of girth control.

....

As I writer I recognise that my life has third act problems.

....

The doctor said to me 'Did you take those tablets I gave you to improve your memory?' I said, 'What tablets?'

Banff is my favourite ski resort that was named by MAD's Don Martin.

Every *Seinfeld* plot would have been solved by a mobile phone.

If I'm on the phone to someone who isn't really listening, I like to suddenly put on a serious voice and say 'You have one hour' and hang up.

My favourite breakup line: I think we should disappoint other people.

My friends just had a baby. It's either got a bottle in its mouth, or it's vomiting. They say it's like living with a 9-pound Uni student.

I'm really struggling to juggle my jobs at the lightbulb, egg, bowling pin, bowling ball, small beanbag, and chainsaw factories.

....

I just got kicked out of a Vans skatewear shop for wearing my baseball cap the right way around.

....

People in movies act like they've never seen a movie.

....

According to Elton John, keep your friends close and your tiny dancers closer.

....

'You need one? Here's fifty.'

  – *Public bathroom hand towel dispensers.*

....

I have an Easter suggestion. Good Friday has a name. We should call the day Jesus rose from the dead Chocolate Sundae.

....

'Instead of joining forces why don't I try until I die, then you try until you die?'

– Mario and Luigi's battle plan.

....

Except for the probable heart attack, it would be funny if the TV finally spoke back to my mother.

....

Researchers say humans used fire as early as one million years ago. They used it to celebrate the release of The Rolling Stones' first album.

....

Hey, guy browsing at the KMart jewellery counter, you're probably closer to finding the cause of your marital problems than the solution.

....

'She loves me, she loves me knot, she loves me...'

– Pirate debating if his wife only likes him for his knotsmanship.

....

NOTE TO SHELF: Hold my books.

....

Know how that song Fever is so sexy?
Last night I had a fever and I shook
violently while trying to eat an SPC fruit
cup. Music lies.

....

HERALD SUN: British actor dies at 79.
Sad, I loved British actor.

....

Alanis Morissette gets more accomplished
during that song with the hand that's not
in her pocket than I do all day with my
entire body.

....

Weird that it's impossible to tickle
yourself but touching your no-no area
feels pretty sweet.

....

My fridge is a retirement home for
fresh produce, where they live out their
last days neglected and alone until they
ultimately perish.

....

I was always a terrible student.
My dog wouldn't even eat my homework.

....

My prison nickname would be 'That Weird
Mouthy Guy Who Got Killed His First Week
In Here'.

....

The 3-hour film *King Kong* was clever.
The first hour meant you could be late
for the movie, the second was great
and the third hour meant you could
leave early.

....

I have a theological question: If God
gets mad and turns your wife into a
pillar of salt, is it OK to use her on
your food or does that just make him
more mad?

....

I think Daisy is a cute name for a kid that's
accident prone because you can nickname
her Whoopsie Daisy.

....

'Mission Control this is, uhh, definitely one of the astronauts... umm... what would you do if a cleaner got stuck on the spacecraft somehow?... over.'

....

I wonder if Sally's parents were like 'Yeah great idea Sally. Sell seashells. On the seashore. Where there are tons of free shells. Idiot.'

....

Despite what the song said, maybe not everybody was Kung Fu fighting.

Maybe some of us were trying to break it up.

....

Just got back from Fight Club. It was really fun! Got there late so missed the rules being read out but I'm sure it was nothing important.

....

My wife said, 'Did you know butterflies only live for two days.' I said, 'I think that's a myth.' She said, 'No, I'm pretty sure it's a butterfly.'

....

I bought my daughter a power fan for her birthday. She was blown away.

....

I just bought some coconut shampoo. I don't know why, though. I don't own a coconut.

....

If you see someone buy an ice cream, a drink and popcorn at the movies, they're a drug dealer. There's no other explanation for that sort of income.

....

I've got mood poisoning.

Must be something I hate.

....

Remember Pat Cash? The best thing about being married to him would be if he got kidnapped and you paid the ransom quick enough you get cash back.

....

Geometry is hard. I tried to quickly draw a square but I ended up with an octagon.

That's what happens when you cut corners.

....

Knock knock.

'Who's there?'

'Dejav.'

'Dejav who?'

Knock knock.

....

A termite goes into a pub. He says to the guy next to him, 'Is the bar tender here?'

....

BOOM

WIFE: 'What was that?'

ME: 'My shirt fell on the ground.'

WIFE: 'It sounded a lot heavier than that.'

ME: 'I was in it.'

....

What's the stupidest animal in the jungle?

The polar bear.

....

I was just looking at my ceiling. Not sure if it's the best ceiling in the world, but it's definitely up there.

....

I managed to burn 1500 calories in 30 minutes!

The pizza was ruined though.

....

These holidays we're having what's called a 'stay-cation.' I didn't want to but the magistrate insisted.

....

I'm jealous of people who use the word 'envious' correctly.

....

You're not boring. I'm only yawning because I'm so interested in your story it's making me tired.

....

The opening title sequence of *Game of Thrones* is longer than the actual episode.

....

The next person that asks me for pineapple juice, cranberry juice, lemonade and a slice of orange in the same glass is gonna get a punch.

....

A bunch of scumbags stole 20 crates of Red Bull from a supermarket yesterday.

I don't know how they sleep at night.

....

The Mexicans are pretty upset about Trump's wall. But they'll get over it.

....

My problem is I have just enough money to get into trouble tonight but not enough money to make bail.

....

When Essendon's coach said at the start of the season he thought they could finish second I didn't realise he meant in every game.

....

'What if I tried to put a ball somewhere and you tried to stop me?'

   – The guy that invented sport.

....

I jumped into the bay with my friends today, even though I didn't want to.

Stupid pier pressure.

....

A photon goes through airport security and is asked if it has any luggage.

The photon says, 'No, I'm travelling light.'

....

Just so we're clear, I am not responsible for what my face does when you talk.

....

Last Xmas I said to my wife, 'I bet you can wrap presents with your eyes shut'.
She said, 'I probably could'.

I said, 'Great, I'll just go and get yours.'

....

Always leave 'Get Well Soon Cards' on the mantel. If you have unexpected guests they'll think you've been too sick to clean.

....

I answered the door today and a 6ft beetle punched me in the face then called me fat and ugly.

Apparently there's a nasty bug going round.

....

A bloke on a tractor just drove past me shouting 'The end of the world is coming!'

I think it was Farmer Geddon.

....

(Enter Password)

Wrong

Wrong

Wrong

(Reset Password)

NEW PASSWORD CANNOT BE OLD PASSWORD

Seriously?

....

Relationships are a lot like algebra.
You look at your X and wonder Y.

....

GENIE: What's your first wish?

DAVE: I wish I was rich.

GENIE: Granted, what's your second wish?

RICH: I want lots of money.

....

The guy who bullied me at school still takes my lunch money. But on the upside, he makes a great Subway footlong.

My daughter bet me I couldn't do a butterfly impression.

I thought to myself, that's got to be worth a flutter.

I hate people that don't understand football but still go along to games to deliberately cause trouble and ruin it for everybody else!

Damn umpires.

I'm trying to explain my car trouble to the mechanic without resorting to sound effects. Nup.

I won't be going to the Logies again. The invitation said 'Black tie only' but when I got there I noticed that other people wore shirts and pants too.

Ex Italian PM Silvio Berlusconi has had his bribery charges dismissed. That was money well spent.

....

A TV repairman has pleaded guilty to burglary and theft. He'll be sentenced next Tuesday between 9:00 am and noon, or between 1:00 pm and 4:00 pm.

....

A man was pulled over after going 70km over the limit. His car was searched and police found a huge bag of amphetamines that he claimed was for his own use. So this guy has been imprisoned for doing excessive speed and for doing excessive speed.

....

A prison inmate accused of killing his ex-wife was left standing alone at the jail-house altar when his new bride-to-be didn't show up for their wedding. He wasn't able to find out what happened to her because he'd used his one phone call to book the caterers.

....

Clothing retailers are being accused of adjusting their change-room mirrors so they make you look thinner. But mirrors don't lie. And luckily for me they don't laugh either.

....

I've been doing this really tough jigsaw puzzle of a rooster. Then my wife came in and told me to put the cornflakes back in the box.

....

It's amazing that eggs don't taste like chicken.

....

I defy anybody using an oxygen mask in a plane emergency to 'continue to breathe normally'.

....

The Grand Prix would be much more interesting if the track wasn't one-way.

....

His name was Mike. I hit him a few times on the top of his head and said, 'Is this thing on?'

....

A prisoner broke out of jail after he sawed his way through bars using dental floss and toothpaste. This escape method is recommended by nine out of 10 prison dentists.

....

I lock the car with the remote. I saw the lights flash, and heard the locks click. Then I press it again because the first time I was an untrustworthy idiot.

....

Knock Knock. Who's there? Orange.
Orange who?
Orange you glad I didn't say moustache?
Actually I probably should have said moustache a few times first. It really helps the joke.

....

Alcoholism is a disease. But it's a pretty good disease because you get to get drunk a lot.

....

Seems the only qualification for getting a taxi license is finding the place where you get taxi licenses.

....

I sprayed mosquito repellent on a mosquito. Now he'll never have any friends.

....

I wonder if there was an award for laziness I could get someone to go pick it up for me?

....

Scientists say there's more bacteria on bank notes than on a toilet so we need to stop paying our plumbers in cash.

....

Bear Grylls is devastated after his sacking by the Discovery Channel. 'Where the hell will I get my weekly fix of antelope pee now?'

....

The Rolling Stones are finally returning to China for some shows. Mick Jagger said, 'I hear they have a wall now.'

....

I've lived in this house for ten years. How come I still don't know which cord makes the blind go up and which one makes it go down? Wrong every time.

....

I just bought my kid a low G.I. Joe.

....

When the night has come. And the land is dark. And the moon is the only light we see. Don't be standing by me. Call the power company.

....

I came access a shop selling camouflage pants. You don't see those much.

....

Ever feel like you're currently living your 'back story' which will be referred to later?

....

I wonder if you can get a semi-colonoscopy?

....

Despite warnings from physicists, organisers are planning to hold an Ironman event on Magnetic Island.

....

Don't you hate people who don't know the difference between 'your' and 'you're'.

There so stupid.

....

You know what they say about cliffhangers...

....

Whenever I go out lately, I'm always followed by a bird with long legs and skinny beak. I think I'm being storked.

....

My wife told me that our son feels neglected.

I didn't even know we had a son.

....

Gambling has brought our family together.

We had to move to a smaller house.

....

A Nigerian Prince has died and left his millions to a cat. He tried to give away his fortune for years, but no one ever responded to his emails.

....

I just slipped on the floor of the local library. I was in the non-friction section.

....

What stands in a paddock and goes
'Oooooh!'?

A cow with no lips.

....

Head and Shoulders shampoo should
make a body wash called Knees
and Toes.

....

Some guy just threw dough, cheese,
salami and tomatoes in my face.
I said, 'You wanna pizza me?'

....

I wonder how the guy who made the first
clock knew what time it was?

....

If you ever feel like your job is meaningless
just remember it's someone's job to fit
indicators to BMWs.

....

You're always told to 'Stay safe. Wear
something bright at night'. The velcro on
this hi-vis vest keeps getting caught on
my doona.

....

The definition of irony:

Not knowing the difference between a definition and an example.

....

I'm kind of glad dinosaurs are extinct because I'm pretty sure I'd try and ride one after I'd had a few drinks.

....

Me and my limbo team go way back.

....

The only time incorrectly isn't spelled incorrectly is when it's spelled incorrectly.

....

Wind farms are ridiculous. As if this country doesn't have enough wind of its own without wasting electricity making more of it by running these big fans.

....

My younger brother was named after my father. That's fine but it's a bit confusing when your brother's called Dad.

....

What's the difference between a candle and a curry?

A candle only burns at one end.

....

For my birthday I got a universal remote control. I thought to myself 'This changes everything.'

....

Last week I replaced every window in my house.

I realised this morning I had a crack in my glasses.

....

Breaking news:

ne ws

....

Do you think horses worry about unicorns like humans worry about aliens?

....

I think landlords who don't allow dogs but DO allow children don't know very much about children.

....

I rang up work this morning.

'My neighbour died last night. I'm going to need some time off work.'

They said 'Sorry for your loss. Take as much time off as you need.'

I said 'Thank you. It'll be about eighteen years, with good behaviour.'

....

I was standing in front of the mirror when my wife walked in.

I said 'I'm bloody huge! Will you help me?'

She said 'Of course' and moved the mirror further away.

....

I have a certain reticence, if reticence is the word, about the word reticence.

....

Facebook is a weapon of mass distraction

....

Coming up next on The Apathetic Gameshow Network, a new episode of The Price is Alright.

....

It's a bird! It's a plane! It's... Superman! And he's... pooping.

Nope, sorry, it's a bird.

....

I am easily the smartest and most attractive person in this compulsive liars support group.

....

The inventor of autocorrect went from zero to hero in a matter of seconds.

....

Doctor, Doctor! Do you think your surname influenced your choice of career?

....

I just try to live my life in such a way that if it ever does flash before my eyes it will be worth watching.

....

Welcome to the 21st century where deleting your history has become more important than making it.

....

I hate going to funerals but I figure if I don't go to other people's funerals, they won't come to mine.

....

The #1 bestselling books are cookbooks and the second are diet books; on how not to eat what you've just learned how to cook.

....

Never go to clubs with metal detectors. I know it feels safe inside, but what about all those guys waiting outside with knives? And they know you haven't got one.

....

What do gardeners do when they retire?

....

Carlton are 500/1 to win the Premiership next year.

Which means if you put just $20 on them at the start of the season, you will lose $20.

....

I came home and found that my daughter was taking drugs. My very best ones, too.

....

I did a gig for Amway. Very wholesome. They use words like 'Cripes'. 'For Cripe's sake.' Who would that be, Jesus Cripe? The son of 'Gosh' and the 'Holy Moly'? I'm not making fun of it. You think I wanna burn in 'Heck'?

....

Sickipedia DONE FROM DEC PC

....

It's my daughter's birthday soon and I went to google 'build a bear' and accidentally googled 'build a bar'. Better idea, I know.

....

People that use big words out of context are just trying to be ambidextrous.

....

I hate it when people call me judgemental. Especially people wearing shoes like that.

....

Q: What's the safest place to be during a North Korean missile strike?

A: The place they're aiming at.

....

I don't like to brag about my cat-like reflexes. That being said, could someone please call for help? I got startled and now I'm stuck up a tree.

....

ME: Why do you involve your friends in all our fights?

HER: That's not true!

TEXT FROM BETH: Yeah, that's not true!

....

Hey Pringles, it's time to widen the can. Your target market customer isn't exactly thin-wristed.

....

I went to the aquarium wearing my cowboy boots and hat.

There's an announcement through the P.A: 'Can we get extra security at the seahorse exhibit? He's here again.'

....

I tried to share a sandwich with a homeless guy today but he told me to bugger off and get my own.

....

We should let prisoners take their own mug shots. We could call it a 'cellfie'.

....

My friend Sid had his id stolen. Now we just call him S.

....

ME: You wanna redeem your anniversary present?

WIFE: The 'One Free Naughty Massage' coupon?

ME: Yes.

WIFE: Sorry, I re-gifted it.

ME: You what? To who?

WIFE: I forgot someone's birthday and I panicked.

ME: TO WHO?!?

WIFE: You may get a weird call from my Auntie.

....

Two clowns were eating a cannibal.
One turns to the other and says, 'Did I start this joke wrong?'

....

Nine out of 10 students agree that someone got lost on the excursion.

....

I hate it when fire trucks drive really slow with their siren on. There's one behind me right now. So annoying.

....

I grew up just a stone's throw away from where that whole family died of mysterious head injuries.

....

Fitness tip: Putting your Fitbit on your dog and letting him run around will get you way more free steps than putting it on your car.

....

What do you call a bulletproof Irishman?
Rick O'Shea.

....

My wife said to me, 'If you could know how and when you were going to die, would you want to know?'
I said, 'No.'
She said, 'OK, forget it.'

....

In the words of Plato, 'I come in four colours, I'm non-toxic and remember to put the lids back on'.

....

Anyone got an owner's manual for a teenage daughter? Mine's giving off a terrible whining noise.

....

My 84-year-old neighbour got the results of his heart test.

They told him the pain in his chest wasn't a heart attack, it was his belt buckle.

....

My wife's been hinting she wants something black and lacy for her birthday. So I've got her a lovely pair of football boots.

....

My friend has been trying for three years to grow a decent moustache. It's slo-mo.

....

When I was younger I had a tough job. I sold 'No hawkers or canvassers' signs, door-to-door.

....

I'll never forget my Grandfather's last words:

'Stop shaking the bloody ladder.'

....

My wife told me to stop singing Wonderwall.

I said, 'Maybe...'

....

I found a Carlton season membership ticket nailed to a tree, so I took it.

You never know when you might need a nail.

....

I went hot air ballooning.

My grandfather invented the cold air balloon but it never really took off.

....

I have this weird talent where I can identify what's inside a wrapped present.

It's a gift.

....

Instead of a swear jar, I have a negativity glass. Every time I have pessimistic thoughts, I put a dollar in.

It's half empty.

'clink'

....

A CURRENT AFFAIR: Can you tell us anything about the asteroid you claim you saw?

ASTRONOMER: No comet.

....

IKEA are in court over a faulty range of luggage. But prosecutors are having a hard time putting a case together.

....

I was on a date and she said to me, 'Do you have any children?'

I said, 'Yes, one that's just under two.'

She said, 'I know how many one is.'

....

My wife kicked me out of the house because my Arnold Schwarzenegger impression was really bad.

But don't worry, I'll return.

....

My cocaine dealer delivers so fast I call him Insta gram.

....

In WW2, my grandfather brought down 18 German fighter planes, killing 54 German aviators.

Worst aircraft mechanic in the Luftwaffe.

....

The first thing I do every morning after I wake up, is make my bed.

Tomorrow I'm returning this piece of crap back to Ikea.

....

I just saw a sign at Coles: 'Turkey: $29'

What a bargain! That's at least a thousand bucks cheaper than Flight Centre.

....

Jokes about communism aren't funny unless everyone gets them.

....

I need to re-home a dog. It's a small terrier, and tends to bark a lot. If you're interested, let me know and I'll jump over our neighbour's fence and get it for you.

....

I am not gullible. I'm just easily tricked which someone told me is very different.

....

I bought a new thesaurus today, but it's nothing to write domicile about.

....

As part of a survey I asked 100 girls what shampoo they prefer to use while they're taking a shower.

They all said the same thing, 'How did you get in here?'

....

You and your child are driving along a deserted road when you come upon a security van full of solid gold bars by the side of the road with the driver dead from a heart attack. What lesson do you teach your child?

Lift with your legs, not your back.

....

My ex texted me, 'Wish you were here.'

She does that every time she walks through a cemetery.

....

If you suck at playing the trumpet,
that's probably why.

....

I woke up in jail. I called the copper over
to my cell. I said, 'Why am I in here?'

He said, 'For drinking.'

I said, 'Great. I'll have a beer.'

....

Turns out Yoda's last name is Layheehoo.

....

How appropriate that the Melbourne
Tunnel Project have named the boring
machines after a politician and a cricketer.

....

Amazon boss Jeff Bezos' wife is leaving
him...

behind the gas meter on the verandah.

....

I asked my wife 'Am I the only one you've
slept with?'

She said, 'Yes, but I've had some fives
and sixes and my first boyfriend was easily
an eight.'

....

When you're dead, you don't know you are dead. It's only painful for others.

The same applies when you're stupid.

....

On a first date:

CLIFF HANGER: 'I've been unlucky in love. I feel like people expect me to be more exciting.'

PAIGE TURNER: 'What a coincidence. I get that too!'

....

I took the kids to feed the ducks.
Turns out ducks don't like the taste of kids.

....

My wife is leaving me because I never put the toilet seat down.

To be honest, I'm not even sure why I started carrying it around with me.

....

A while ago I went to see my doctor.
She said 'Don't eat anything fatty.'

I said, 'You mean like bacon and sausage?'

She said, 'No fatty. Don't eat anything.'

....

How to prepare perfect Brussels sprouts:

1) Half fill a pot with water and bring to the boil.
2) Add a little salt.
3) Cut off the stem end of the sprout and remove any yellowing outer leaves.
4) Cut a cross in the base of each sprout.
5) Carefully place sprouts in the bin.

....

I just bought some bathers with Doritos printed on them. I'm going for a dip later.

....

Knock knock?

Who's there?

Biggish

Biggish who?

No thanks but here's $5.

....

I started up a dating site for chickens but had to give it up because I was struggling to make hens meet.

....

Our local shopping strip has really changed. We've got an new optometrist, a new carpet emporium and a new bakery.

It used to be cool but now it's all specs, rugs and sausage rolls.

....

...and the award for best lead actress in a dramatic role goes to my daughter for 'I Have An Earache, Why Don't You Care That I'm Dying?'

....

I just bought some state-of-the-art garden shears.

They're the latest in cutting hedge technology.

....

I used to work in a Russian napkin factory. I was the shop steward.

I was in the serviette union.

....

Whoever said laughter is the best medicine clearly hasn't tried curing diarrhoea with a tickle fight.

....

We're so skint in our house, the wife had to sell one of her kidneys to pay for the kid's new school uniform.

If it gets any worse I'm gonna have to cancel Foxtel Sports.

....

A bloke is walking along the footpath, dragging his foot along the ground.
He notices another man walking towards him dragging his foot too.

As the two men pass, one points at his foot and says 'Vietnam 50 years back'.

The second man points down at his and says, 'Dog poo, 50 yards back'.

....

How to start an argument on Facebook:

1) Express an opinion.

2) Wait.

....

I was drinking coffee in my slippers this morning when I thought to myself, I really need to wash some mugs.

....

The Romaine empire has fallen.
Cos Caesar is dead.

Lettuce pray.

....

They reckon that there are no such things
as problems, only opportunities.

So apparently I have a serious drinking
opportunity.

....

I just discovered that the word 'nothing'
is a palindrome.

Backwards it spells 'gnihton', which also
means nothing.

....

A good way to find out if you're old is to
fall down in front of a group of people.
If they laugh, you're young. If they panic,
you're old.

....

I wanted to do really well in my wasp
collecting exam.

But I got a bee.

....

(During an interview): 'Do you have any questions?'

ME: 'Yeah, in *Titanic* why did Jack sink when he died but everyone else floated?'

....

I bet I know why aliens don't visit our solar system.

They've looked at the reviews and we only have one star.

....

We were at the beach and my wife asked for me to bring her something hard to write on.

I brought her a handful of sand. Sand is pretty hard to write on.

....

Red sky at night: sailor's delight.

Blue sky at night: day.

....

I have a bumper sticker on my car that says, 'Honk if you think I'm sexy'.

Sometimes I just sit at green lights until I feel good about myself.

....

They say that time is a great healer.

That explains why you have to wait a week to get a doctor's appointment.

....

'Dad, can we go to McDonald's?'

'We can if you can spell it.'

'Forget it. Let's go to KFC.'

....

I was feeling lonely, so I bought some shares.

It's nice to have some company.

....

My stamp collection has really taken off since I stopped mailing letters.

....

I made a rocking chair in woodwork class.

It wasn't meant to rock, I'm just terrible at woodwork.

....

My neighbour has just come back after two weeks away in Perth, so there were huge celebrations. In Perth.

....

I went to a temporary tattoo studio yesterday to get a tattoo.

It wouldn't wash off this morning, so I went back to complain, but the tattoo studio wasn't there.

....

I finally got the book I'm writing on clocks completed.

It's about time.

....

I had a vasectomy because I didn't want any kids.

But when I got home, they were still there.

....

I was at the mechanic.

'My car makes a funny noise. Listen.'

'Sir, that's the horn.'

....

I am NOT a stalker. But you should call your mum. She left you a message yesterday while you were sleeping. I muted it so you could rest.

....

They say 'Love like you've never been hurt, dance like nobody's watching and work like you don't need the money.'

I say 'Work like nobody's watching, love like you don't need the money and dance like someone's really gonna get hurt'.

....

One time when I was younger I got fired for being too drunk. Not for being drunk. For being TOO drunk.

I miss that place.

....

My wife crashed her car this morning.

When the police came, she said the other guy involved was on his mobile and eating a pie at the time.

The police told her the man was entitled to do what he wanted in his own house.

....

Someone is stealing cats in our suburb. I hope that the police catch the purr purr traitor.

....

My mate is the biggest Beatles fan in the world. He's obsessed. He's got every single they ever recorded except one.

I think he needs Help.

....

I like to be frank when I talk to women. I prefer they don't know my real name.

....

I gave myself a prostate exam this morning.

That's the last time I buy toilet paper from the Vic Market.

....

Brunos are from Mars, Freddies are from Mercury.

....

If I was a giraffe, I'd get a neck tattoo of the Empire State Building.

....

MY WIFE: 'Paul is coming over.'

ME: 'Paul from work or Paul who is good at disguises?'

MY WIFE: 'Paul who – *(pulls off wife mask)* – is good at disguises!'

....

Comedian father clutches his chest.

'Son, call me an ambulance.'

COMEDIAN SON: 'Umm, you're...
    an ambulance?'

COMEDIAN FATHER: '...p...p...proud of you.'

Dies.

....

The newlywed couple laughed when
I gave them blankets labeled 'his' and
'hers'.

Obviously this is their first marriage.

....

Whenever I feel discouraged, I remember
the words of my then three-year-old after
she vomited carrots on the floor:

'I'm gonna need more carrots.'

....

Going out with someone based solely
on their looks is so shallow. You should
consider other things, like do they have
a lot of money?

....

A British guy just complained to me about how it's not fair that all the other countries have an independence day and England doesn't.

....

ME: *(to my crime gang)* Let's ditch our getaway car in this lake.

(I put a rock on the accelerator and car revs into the lake, disappearing underwater.)

ME: OK now... wait what's that splashing?

(The car emerges from the water on the far shore and just keeps going.)

NARRATOR: The all new Toyota Kluger...

....

'I hate going to these posh restaurants. I can never pronounce anything on the menu.'

– *Me, drunk, holding the Pancake Parlour menu upside down.*

....

Congratulations to the person that invented the wobbly restaurant table because it's basically everywhere now.

....

On a lonely walking trail I came upon a lady in labour about to give birth so I stopped to help.

ME: 'Keep pushing! I can see the head!'

LADY: 'That's MY head. You're at the wrong end.'

....

Our neighbour has identical twin three-year-old girls. They each have a sippy cup with their names on them. When she's not looking, I switch the cups.

....

I bet you $14,560 you can't guess how much I owe my bookie.

....

When you do squats, are your knees supposed to sound like a goat chewing on an aluminium can stuffed with celery?

....

Home Alone is a movie that explains how child neglect and bad parenting is hilarious.

....

ME: A pessimist sees the glass half empty; an optimist see the glass half full.

WIFE: *(returning from the toilet)* Why is half my milkshake gone?

ME: Because you're a pessimist.

....

My friends call me 'Captain Compromise'. It wasn't my first choice for a nickname but I can live with it.

....

We'll We'll We'll,

if it isn't autocorrect.

....

How the worm got its name:

'Hey what's that squiggly thing on the ground?'

'I don't know, depending on which side you're looking at it from, it looks kinda like a w or m.'

....

I've never been offered money for sex. But I've never been offered money to not have sex either. So at least there's that.

....

If I could have dinner with anyone, alive or dead, I'm pretty sure I'd want to be alive.

....

I've got 99 problems, and being upside down is one of them.

Actually wait, I've got 66 problems.

....

DAUGHTER: What's a sex tape?

ME: A sex tape? Um, well when, um, two people have, um, when they're attracted to each other they...

DAUGHTER: Dad, I know what sex is. What's a tape?

....

I need to hire a proorfreader.

....

HOW DO I CONVINCE EVERYONE THAT I'M NOT SHOUTING WHEN I EXPLAIN THAT MY CAT STOLE MY CAPS LOCK KEY?

....

You had me at 'we have a warrant'.

....

Growing up with a dyslexic father had its advantages. Whenever he caught me swearing, he used to wash my mouth out with soup.

....

Read It and Weep: A Book on How to Cry.

....

I was at the post office today to pay a bill and there was a guy in the queue holding a gift wrapped parcel. There is one business day left before Christmas.
I thought to myself, 'Fat chance, unless that gift is for someone who works at this post office.'

....

Divorcee's gift idea:

A T-shirt saying, 'I'm not with Stupid any more'.

....

I opened a bottle of wine to let it breathe. It didn't. So I gave it mouth to mouth.

....

Just looking for some guidance here. If you're an onlooker at a car crash, a fire or similar, how many metres back do you have to be before it's okay to snack on potato chips?

....

I bet Medusa's husband got sick of pulling a wad of snakes out the plug hole whenever the shower blocked up.

....

If no one comes from the future to stop you from doing it then how bad of a decision can it really be?

....

My wife said she wanted Chanel No.5 for her birthday.

She's going to be happy. All I had to do was re-tune the TV.

....

How's this for irony? While I was buying the new version of Grand Theft Auto, someone stole my car.

....

If you get a gift from me, there may or may not be a pair of scissors between the wrapping and the gift. Anyways, I'm gonna need those back.

....

I'm running out of time to be a 'trophy husband' so now I think I'd be happy with a 'I finished the race' husband.

....

My daughter finally cleaned her room.

I said, 'You better not have just thrown everything in your wardrobe.'

She said, 'I didn't.'

I said, 'Good.'

She said, 'I threw it in your wardrobe.'

....

At a job interview.

BOSS: You're asking for a pretty high salary considering you have no experience in this field.

ME: I know but this job is going to be really hard because I have no experience in this field.

....

When my daughter was four:

ME: What sound does a cow make?

HER: Moooo.

ME: Good, a duck?

HER: Quack.

ME: Good, how about a seal?

HER: My power my PLEASURE
   MY PAIN, babaaaayyy.

ME: Good.

....

I bought an ornamental lamp post for
my garden but it keeps getting stolen
so I've chained it to a bicycle.

....

My Auntie had a rather shrill phone voice.
I once spent 20 minutes talking to her
before realising it was actually someone
trying to send us a fax.

....

Bank robbers are never mothers.

'OK, EVERYONE GET ON THE GODDAMN
FLOOR!! No, wait, get up. You'll get dirty.'

....

I dropped in on my daughter's maths club dinner. They had pi.

....

I'm at a costume party. I've just won eight straight games of rock, paper, scissors against Edward Scissorhands.

....

My Grandfather was a baker in the army.

He went in all buns glazing.

....

Robert Frost's notes.

FINAL DRAFT: Two roads diverged in a wood and I took the one less travelled.

FIRST DRAFT: Two roads diverged in a wood and I took the one on the left because the one on the right looked muddy and I had nice new shoes on.

....

After last year's fatalities the Zoo have decided to cancel this year's 'Jumanji Day'.

....

From now on I'll be writing all my jokes in capitals.

This one was written in Canberra.

....

I'm giving away free contradictions for $1.

....

Christmas shopping:

SALESGIRL: Can I help you, sir?

ME: Yes. I'd like a nice dress to give to my wife for Christmas that she can exchange on Boxing Day.

....

Those in-door refrigerator ice dispensers are perfect for those times when you need either zero or 5000 ice cubes.

....

I'm watching TV but I'm sick of the censor's 'beep, beep' right through the show. I'm old enough to know what the Road Runner is really saying.

....

The other day my teenage daughter said to us, 'Mum, Dad, I've decided to live on my own.'

We said, 'Ha. Okay.'

She said, 'Cool. Your luggage is outside.'

....

A Quick Guide on how to fall down a flight of stairs:

Step 1

Step 2

Step 6

Steps 9, 10, 11

....

I saw a spider in the shower. I was like, 'Oh jeez I'm sorry, but lock the door next time, buddy.'

....

I can make great ice cream.

I learnt at sundae school.

....

I'm chasing a dog on my bike. I can't understand how he's even reaching the pedals.

....

The gingerbread man goes to the doctor.

GINGERBREAD MAN: Doc, my knee hurts.

DOCTOR: Have you tried icing it?

....

The 50-50-90 rule: Anytime you have a 50-50 chance of getting something right, there's a 90% chance you'll get it wrong.

....

I imagine the worst part about being sober is you have to blame your bad decisions on just being an idiot.

....

The new trend is people writing their own funny obituary. I hope that's why people keep telling me they can't wait to read my obituary.

....

What idiot made up head over heels in love? Aren't we ALWAYS head over heels?

....

Plastic surgery = tailoring your birthday suit.

....

Is heaven BYO harp? Need to know ASAP.

....

What's the best wine to pair with crippling feelings of inadequacy? Oh, that's right – any wine.

....

I'm a great athlete, and an even better liar!

....

I haven't met the new guy 'Carl' but I like him already because this sandwich with his name on it from the office fridge is delicious.

....

A lozenge would have ended Rod Stewart's career.

....

My uncle was an Elvis impersonator. He didn't sing like him or look like him but he did die on the toilet.

....

Meditation is a chance for me to sit still and let my thoughts attack me.

....

If you ever encounter a crocodile in the Northern Territory, play dead. If you're not sure what dead looks like, just wait a couple of minutes.

....

Nostalgia was better when I was younger.

....

I'm glad Christmas Caroling season is over. My voice is shot. I spent all December yelling at Christmas carolers to shut the hell up.

....

There's nothing less relaxing than when someone tells you, 'Relax.'

....

I read that Vincent Van Gogh wasn't recognized in his lifetime. How many one eared guys were there back then?

....

Sometimes I'll eat a certain food just to see what it does to my poo.

....

Thump the side of your cat with your palm like it's a dog and the cat will look at you like, 'Hey, what's the big idea?!' Funny.

....

I can't eat Black Forest Cake without worrying about what I'm doing to the environment.

....

In L.A. I'm going to be staying in Echo Park or as it's known locally, 'Echo Park, Echo Park.'

....

Insanity is doing the same thing, over and over again, and not working on an assembly line.

....

I can't watch the movie *Se7en* until I watch Se1en through Se6en.

....

Wizard Home Loans have signed a sponsorship deal with Parramatta. They've said they expect the team to go out there and give 3.95 per cent.

....

Don't insult my intelligents.

....

You'd think 'Your eyes look so pretty when you roll them' would be a great pick up line.

....

I've had it up to here with gesticulating.

....

You have no idea how hard it is to find a greeting card for your wife that says, 'I don't remember where I left the baby.'

....

I need a job that pays well and requires me to do very little. How do I become a Kardashian?

....

Farting in the taxi makes the driver get you to your destination the fastest.

....

I like to believe that the ATM is laughing 'with' me.

....

Today I feel 'medical supply catalogue model' pretty.

....

Fashion tip: look bored.

....

Witnessing a public break-up is a million times better than your favourite TV show.

....

I told my wife, 'You can't die in a dream.'

She said, 'What are you talking about?
You die in my dreams all the time.'

....

I couldn't afford a trip to Europe,
so I just went backpacking through IKEA
and it took longer.

....

It's been three weeks since my friend
passed away and he still hasn't updated
his Facebook status to say whether he's
in heaven or hell.

....

I hope I look as good as Keith Richards
does when I've been dead for two years.

....

'The Bachelor' is being sued for
discrimination. Against the intelligent.

....

I'm starting a support group for recovering
computer hackers called Anonymous
Anonymous.

....

I had to stop doing yoga because it was stressing me out.

....

People buying yellow cars better be getting a discount.

....

Using a remote control is the closest most of us get to being wizards.

....

You and I are the type of people who could be given the gift of immortality, and still manage to find a way to die.

....

Bond villains always seem really good with money. I wish they would give investment advice.

....

Some people meditate to forget. I forget to meditate.

....

The tattooist said to me that she didn't believe in anaesthetic. I said, 'I assure you, it does exist'.

....

Honey, I bought a new door because
I think we should see other peep-hole.

....

I wonder how people who work for
LinkedIn got their jobs.

....

At what age does Ryan Gosling have
to change his name to Ryan Goose?

....

There's no life on earth without water.
Because without water there's no coffee.
And without coffee I'll kill you all.

....

I feel like tear gas would really help me
express my emotions.

....

I love it when someone's laugh is funnier
than the joke.

....

Just so you don't waste your time, a
serious response to a joke Facebook
post has never 'taught anyone a lesson'.

....

If mustard could get leprosy, that's what my neighbour's house smells like.

....

Slow wifi is worse than no wifi at all.

....

The correct serving size for guacamole is 'until you run out of chips'.

....

My footsteps are one million times louder when I'm sneaking.

....

If you could see all the other people who drank at a water fountain before you, no one would ever drink at a water fountain.

....

I'd be more of a fan of exercising if calories screamed when you burned them.

....

Women are fascinated by mythical creatures like unicorns, vampires, and men who are good listeners.

....

Volleyball is just a more intense version of 'don't let the balloon touch the floor'.

....

People who can fall asleep quickly freak me out. Don't they have thoughts?

....

Some people are as useless as the 'ay' in 'okay'.

....

Do you think Willy Wonka still used that chocolate after the kid had nearly drowned in it?

....

I just want to thank my mailman for delivering my recycling directly to my house.

....

I named my law firm/night club 'Mullet'. People will have to walk through the business in the front to get to the party in the back.

....

Billion-dollar idea: An app that sends you a text when the light turns green.

....

When standing in line, I only hate the people in front of me. Everyone behind me is cool.

....

'Let's see how unpopular we can get.'

 – *Politicians.*

....

In ten years, guy's jeans will be so tight they'll wear them on the inside of their body.

....

'I'm not that type of guy.'

 – *That type of guy.*

....

Nobody in a Ford Focus is on their way to get a knuckle tattoo.

....

Rich people like eating outdoors more than poor people do.

....

If the '80s taught me anything it's that steel workers are also very good at dancing and gymnastics.

....

You know when a tough guys say 'I'm the last person you wanna mess with'? Well I'm the first person you so wanna mess with.

....

Steve Buscemi is what would happen if a foot could sneeze.

....

Is it too late to start calling shampoo 'hair soap'?

....

I'm gonna stop being so pessimistic. It's never gonna work out.

....

I'm proud that not wearing a watch has never stopped me from looking at my wrist when people ask me what time it is.

....

Have fun at the playground in McDonald's tonight, single dads.

....

I hope I never have to explain to a time travelling nine-year-old me why I spend more money on ties than roller coasters.

....

You don't have to specify 'Dog, the Bounty Hunter'. You're the only guy named Dog. We hear 'Dog' we get who they're talking about.

....

Apply for a job at the Deed Poll office if you want to make a name for yourself.

....

Theme parks are valuable research into the effects of long queues on sugar-filled children, cleverly disguised as fun.

....

Find out if a relationship is worth pursuing by going to Couples Therapy for your first date.

....

Before you judge someone, walk a mile in their shoes. Unless they own a shoe shop because you'll be arrested for shoplifting.

....

All sports teams nicknamed 'Cougars' now have a player's mum as the mascot.

....

The man who invented the Wurlitzer has died. He refused to donate his organs because he wants his kids to take over the business.

....

Save on washing up time by putting your dinner on a frisbee and then throwing it next door when you're finished.

....

If I was on a board of directors I'd make the youngest member wear a Baby On Board sticker.

....

Don't judge a book by its cover. Unless it's a book about how to make good first impressions with your appearance.

....

I saw a film about my fear of flying. It's called Shakes On A Plane.

....

I say my bedroom is where the magic happens because I spend most of my time there doing card tricks.

....

If you have to fire someone, soften the blow by giving them a 'Sorry You're Leaving' card and changing it to 'Sorry. You're Leaving!!'

....

The last fifty years of the working day really drag on, don't they?

....

'I can't go to a party without getting completely smashed.'– Greek dinner plate.

....

If you're offered a sales job at farm, it will be largely field-based.

....

Keep your party guests on their toes by putting all their belongings on a high shelf.

....

'Ask me no questions, I'll tell you no lies' is a good caveat, but not a great way to start a job interview.

....

If you're interviewing for an accountancy position, do not promise to give 110%.

....

Have you noticed since everyone has a phone camera these days nobody talks about seeing UFOs like they used to?

....

Rich people stay rich by living like they're broke. Broke people stay broke by living like they're rich.

....

I was audited. The tax officer tells me I owe 30 grand. I opened my briefcase and gave him 30 grand in cash. He starts to write out a receipt. I said, 'I just gave you 30 grand cash and you're gonna put it through the books?'

....

I went to the baggage counter to complain about my lost luggage and the guy came out to the desk wearing my pants.

....

The first thing you learn in the outback is never pat a snake on the head. If you do, the last thing you learn is never pat a snake on the head.

....

I got some of that 'I can't believe it's not butter' and mixed it with real butter. Now I have a tub of 'I can believe some of this is butter'.

....

I love digital cameras because they allow you to reminisce immediately. 'Look at us there. So young. Where do the seconds go?'

....

Language is funny. Saying 'I'm sorry' is the same as saying, 'I apologise'.

Unless you're at the guy's funeral.

....

'Sort of' is a fairly harmless thing to say. It doesn't really mean anything. But there are times when it can mean everything. Like after, 'I love you', or 'You're going to live', or 'It's a boy'.

....

I'm not a big fan of Tiger Airlines. Before we took off the captain asked the passengers to chip in for the fuel.

....

Wouldn't it be cool if you were writing a ransom note on your computer and that paper clip popped up and said, 'Looks like you're writing a ransom note. Would like some help with that? You should swear more, you'll get more money.'

....

I don't buy autobiographies. I just flip to the 'About the Author' section. Done. Next?

....

I was in Alaska. I played golf in the snow. My caddy was a moose. Every time I reached for a club, he thought I was trying to steal his antlers.

....

I think foosball, you know, table soccer, is a combination of soccer and shish kebabs. Foosball screwed up my perception of soccer. I thought you had to kick the ball then spin round and round. I can't do a back flip. Much less several. Simultaneously with two other guys. That look just like me.

....

The Wright brothers invented flying. Orville Wright said to his brother, 'You were only in the air twelve seconds. How could my luggage be in Cairo?'

....

Got a phone call today to do a gig at a fire station. I went along. Turned out it was a hoax.

....

My car radio got stolen. The insurance company sent me a form saying they needed to know what kind of radio it was so they can reimburse me. I couldn't remember what it was so I tried to think of a really expensive sounding brand. They rang me a week later saying they didn't think Rolex made radios. I told them it was a clock radio.

....

Clairvoyants association cancelled due to unforeseen circumstances but I met a gypsy there, and she's reading my future in a crystal ball. 'I see a man with a large forehead and small chin'. I said, 'That's my reflection'. She said, 'Silence, do not mock the ball. Now, I can see you are Cambodian, no Canadian, no you are a custodian'. I said, 'No, I'm a comedian. Do you have spell check on that ball?'

....

Q. What does Australian bowler Mitchell Johnson put in his hands to make sure the next ball almost always takes a wicket?

A. A bat.

....

My wife and I were lying in bed and our neighbour's dog was barking like mad in their backyard. Finally I said, 'To hell with this!' and stormed out of the bedroom.
I came back five minutes later and my wife said, 'What did you do?'
I said, 'I've put the dog in our backyard. Let's see how they like it!'

....

I bought a cuckoo clock at the Army disposals store. Last night at ten, the bird chirped twenty two hundred times.

....

When I was five we had to move because dad sold our house. Somehow the landlord found out about it and we had to move.

....

A Canadian psychologist is selling a DVD that teaches you how to test your dog's IQ. Here's how it works: if you spend twenty bucks for the DVD, your dog is smarter than you.

....

My friend lives on Magnetic Island. He'd leave but he's got a metal plate in his head.

....

You pull over and put your left blinker on, have to double park so you put your hazards on, get out, get back in, drive off and hear your blinker so you turn it off but you still hear it so you turn it off again actually putting the right blinker on then see the hazard indicator on so you turn them off but leaving your right blinker on. You see it and turn it off. The guy behind you is like, 'Where the hell is this guy going?'

....

My grandpa was old. He had his prostate checked by an archaeologist. They found cave paintings and an arrowhead.

....

I went to the National Geographic store and bought the world's oldest globe. It's flat.

....

I got so drunk I did the smart thing and took a bus home. Which was impressive because I'd never driven a bus before.

....

I'm writing the life story of my car. It's an auto-biography.

....

A guy walks into my front yard and stops face to face with my Rottweiler. He says, 'Is that dog safe?' I said, 'He's a hell of a lot safer than you are.'

....

My daughter gave me a cloth calendar. It took me three hours to embroider a dental appointment.

....

We're very proud of our national heritage. The Eureka Stockade captured the very spirit of our young country. And you can capture that spirit yourself with this patriotic Eureka Stockade chess set from Franklin Mint. That's right, for only $79.99 plus postage and handling Franklin Mint will send you one piece every month so you can finally settle down for that chess game in about five years. And each piece is sent for your approval. Like you're not gonna want them all. 'I don't think I'll need all the pawns. They get lost and they don't do much. And I think I can get by with just the one Bishop.' And remember this is a strictly limited release. We'll only make them till a guy drops and breaks the mould at the lead factory in China.

....

My parents hated giving me bad news.
They'd never tell me a pet died. Once
I woke up and my goldfish was gone.
I said, 'Where's Goldy?' They said,
'He ran away'.

....

I'm addicted to placebos. I'd quit but it
wouldn't matter.

....

The universe is expanding. That should
help ease the traffic.

....

I often wonder if my life would have been
different if I'd been born one day earlier.
Probably not except I would have asked
that question yesterday.

....

I watched a war movie where the
defence department bought some cheap
submarines made out of styrofoam and
they wouldn't go under the water.

....

I had an MRI to find out if I have
claustrophobia.

....

I'm taking vitamins but you have to swallow so many before you feel full.

....

We all have string. Every house has some string hanging around but you never see ads for string. 'Try our string. It's great. It's almost rope.'

....

My teacher was nearly deaf so he used to turn the heating way down in the classroom so if anybody asked anything he could see who was talking.

....

They found out who killed the Boston strangler. The Boston strangler strangler.

....

Nevada has voted against legalised marijuana. They felt it would send the wrong message to Nevada's young gamblers and prostitutes.

....

Dave drowned. So at the funeral we got him a wreath in the shape of a lifebelt. Well, it's what he would have wanted.

....

Imagine if birds were tickled by feathers you'd see a flock of seagulls flying past laughing hysterically.

....

When I proposed it was very romantic. I turned off the TV. Well, I muted it. During a commercial.

....

My first wife, when we got married she changed her name. I know that's old fashioned; she changed her name. But she wouldn't tell me what it was.

....

Marriage is a contract. No it's not. Contracts come with a warrantee. A guarantee that if there's a problem you can take me back to the manufacturer. You can't do that in a marriage. You gonna take me back to my parent's house? 'He's broke. He doesn't work.'

....

A man in Darwin nearly died when he kissed his pet tiger snake on the lips. When he got to hospital his condition was listed as serious but it was later upgraded to stupid.

....

I'm not a fighter, I have bad reflexes.
I got run over by a car being pushed
by two guys.

....

Think of how stupid the average person
is, and realise half of us are stupider
than that.

....

I love curries. I keep my toilet paper in
the fridge.

....

I owe the tax department 80 grand. I rang
them and said, 'How much for cash?'

....

There's a girl at an airport bar. She looked
like a flight attendant so I thought I'd get
her attention by singing her airline jingle
but I didn't know what airline she was with
so I'm trying a few. 'I've been to cities...'
Nothing. 'Singapore girl, you're a great
way to fly...' Nope. 'Fly Malaysia...' No.
She turns to me and says, 'Will you just
piss off!!' I said, 'Ah, Tiger.'

....

When the Earl of Sandwich died they
buried him between two other guys.

....

My grandfather's trousers kept creeping higher and higher each year. By the time he was 80 he was just a pair of pants and a head.

....

Employee of the month is a good example of how somebody can be both a winner and a loser at the same time.

....

If you're being chased by a police dog, try not to go through a tunnel, then on to a little seesaw, then jump through a hoop of fire. They're trained for that.

....

I have a couple of horses, and one of them broke his leg so I had to shoot it. So now it has a broken leg and a gunshot wound. I'm not sure why they tell you to shoot them when they break their leg. Must help in the healing process. If it's not better by next week, I'm gonna shoot it again.

....

I'm a strange guy. I'm allergic to cotton wool. I have pills I'm supposed to take but I can't get them out of the bottle.

....

Scientists have announced that the sun is only five billion years old. It just looks older because it's spent so much time in the sun.

....

I was driving my car and had a smash with a magician. The guy came out of nowhere.

....

Super model Naomi Campbell was slapped with an eight million-dollar law suit for allegedly smacking her secretary in the head with a telephone. Experts say she that could have saved two million dollars if she'd been with Optus.

....

I made out my will the other day, and I'm in it. If I die, I get everything.

....

My grandfather used to say to me, 'Don't watch your money, watch your health'. Then one day, while I was watching my health, someone stole my money. It was my grandfather.

....

People always say stuff like 'He died penniless' like it was a bad thing. Sounds like good timing to me.

....

I was in a trophy shop with my friend, and there were trophies everywhere. My friend looks around and whispers, 'This guy is REALLY good.'

....

At a karaoke bar in Japan, a man who booed a singer's version of 'My Way' was killed by the singer and his friend. Witnesses called it the best Frank Sinatra impression they'd ever seen.

....

Most hotel keys are now the size and shape of credit cards. One night I got back to my hotel room and accidentally used my Visa card. The next month I got billed for a hotel door.

....

People have too many food allergies in Australia. It's because we have too much food. Do you think there's anybody in Ethiopia who's gluten free or lactose intolerant?

....

Christmas always sucked at my house
because I believed in Santa Claus.
Unfortunately, so did my parents,
so I never got anything.

....

I like beer. Sometimes I will drink beer
to celebrate a major event like the fall of
the Berlin Wall or the fact my refrigerator
is still working.

....

Cutting funds to the SETI program,
American politicians have said they've
found no signs of intelligent life on other
planets. Aliens have responded by saying
they've found no signs of intelligent life in
American politics.

....

Did you see the story of two baby wombats
are being hand-reared at an animal shelter
in Wonthaggi after their mothers were
both hit by early morning milk trucks?
The babies are being fed three bottles
of milk a day. Talk about rubbing it in.

....

President Trump told our PM that Australia is America's closest ally. But he recently said the same thing to the French about France, the Canadians about Canada, the Germans about Germany and the Brits about Britain. So to sort it out, all these countries will now go to war to see which place America actually helps.

....

There are rumours coming out of Hollywood that police allegedly discovered Charlie Sheen doing cocaine with two prostitutes. But Charlie Sheen's agent has said the actor was just researching his new movie role, 'The Charlie Sheen Story'.

....

A duck hunter has been shot by his dog that allegedly trod on the man's rifle, discharging it. But police became suspicious after CCTV footage showed the dog earlier in the day at a nearby hotel accepting money from two ducks.

....

The man who invented Christmas decorations has died. He will be buried in the top closet for eleven months of the year.

....

A local scientist has discovered how to take the bitterness out of cumquats. He's now working on taking the arrogance out of bananas.

....

Thieves have stolen an elite swimmer's Olympic and Commonwealth Games medals which certainly seems easier than all that training.

....

Cheetah, the monkey from the Tarzan movies, has died at the age of 80. The relatives of the late star are now in a bitter dispute over his estate, which includes a tyre swing and his prized collection of rubber bananas.

....

Nicotine patches are under review after studies showed they're not very effective in stopping smoking and can be as addictive as cigarettes. A northern suburbs mother confused her husband's patches for Band-Aids and put them on her child's grazed knee. The kid's now got a twenty graze a day habit.

....

A new cosmetic skin cream is on the way that tricks human skin cells into regenerating themselves. It's based on an earlier skin cream that tricked people into buying the earlier skin cream.

....

Research has shown that I'm less likely to catch a cold if I walk regularly but six times more likely to catch a cold if I run a marathon. I'd probably catch it from the person giving me mouth to mouth.

....

Unfit Australians are using the Wii video game system to exercise in their own living rooms. The most popular games are Wii Cycling Tour, Wii Olympic Marathon and Wii MICA Cardiac Paramedic.

....

Our local public transport system was thrown into chaos on Monday when an unusually high number of train drivers called in sick. The most common complaint was they were sick of being train drivers.

....

There's a new high-priced high-tech fridge on the way here that will tell you if you've run out of something or where it is in the fridge. This would eliminate the huge inconvenience of opening the door.

....

Imagine if birds were tickled by feathers. You'd see a flock of seagulls fly by laughing hysterically.

....

I found a snake in my yard and got a shovel and whacked the hell out of it. Then I didn't have Foxtel for a week.

....

An aquarium is like a lava lamp with poo.

....

My car has this feature that I guess is standard on all cars, because my last car had it too. It has a rotating petrol tank. Whatever side of the pump I pull up to, it's on the other side.

....

I was at Not Quite Right Pets. I bought a faulty cat that only had five lives.

....

If the car had followed the same development path as the computer, a Rolls Royce would cost a thousand dollars, get a million miles to the gallon and explode once a year for no reason, killing everyone inside.

....

I'm having car problems. Those warning lights on the dash come on a lot. Yesterday I saw the 'check oil' light. Then the 'Check engine' light came on. I couldn't check the engine, there was too much smoke. Then the 'game over' light came on. That was a new one.

....

My childhood was kind of a blur. I needed better glasses.

....

I was a boring kid. When we played doctor, they always made me the anaesthesiologist.

....

Having children gives your life purpose. Currently my purpose is to get some sleep.

....

My wife is about to have our second
child, and we're very happy because
we were told we couldn't have kids.
By our landlord.

....

I had to work to put myself through Uni.
I sold encyclopaedias door to door.
When the college librarian found out,
she was pretty mad.

....

My last credit card bill was so big, before
I opened it I actually heard a drum roll.

....

Police have just caught Australia's
first female serial killer. She got eight
men. But she didn't kill them. She broke
into their homes and hid their TV remote
controls, so they killed themselves.

....

The law is stupid. If a burglar breaks
into your home and you shoot him,
he can sue you.

For what, restraint of trade?

....

When my daughter gets to high school, she can go out with the captain of the chess team. Any guy that takes three hours to make a move is fine by me.

....

I went to the doctor. He said, 'Say ahhh'. I said, 'Why?' He said, 'My dog died.'

....

They've found out that nine out of ten dentists think that one out of ten dentists is an idiot.

....

Remember folks, in the city those traffic lights timed for 50kph are also timed for 100kph.

....

I drove a cab while I was at Uni. I never picked anybody up. I just needed a car.

....

An escalator can never break down. It can only become stairs. You should never see an 'Escalator temporarily out of order' sign. Just 'Escalator temporarily stairs. Sorry for the convenience'.

....

If you want to lose weight you have to exercise. I joined the gym. They had this new machine there called the Nautilus. I couldn't figure out how to work it, so I just strapped it on and dragged it around the gym. I'm up to five machines now.

....

I did a gig at a politician's kid's party. We played 'Pin the blame on the donkey'.

....

Fashion is great in autumn because earth tones are back in, which means I don't have to do the laundry as often.

....

I had goldfish because they say looking at fish is relaxing. That's why I always doze off when I'm snorkelling.

....

At the airport they asked me if anybody I didn't know gave me anything. Even the people I know don't give me anything.

....

If carrots are so good for your eyes, how come I see so many dead rabbits on the highway?

....

Australians spend fifty billion dollars a year on games of chance. And that doesn't include weddings and elections.

....

If you put a government agency in charge of the Gibson Desert, it would run out of sand.

....

Insurance sucks. There's always conditions. My accident policy covers me for falling off the roof but not hitting the ground.

....

I never saw the movie, *Independence Day*. Ironically, I didn't want to go by myself.

....

Have you seen that TV show, 'Hypothetical?' OK, let's just suppose for a moment that you had.

....

I think the fleas at my house have got military training. I set off a flea bomb and they diffused it.

....

I was reading how the female spider will eat the male spider after mating. I guess female spiders know that insurance is easier to collect than child support.

....

Donald Trump says he named his daughter after his favourite store. I was just talking about that to my two kids, Kay and Mart.

....

I did a gig at a restaurant for single people. No tables or chairs. Forty people eating while standing over a sink.

....

I'm learning karate. If I focus all my spiritual energy, I can break my hand with a brick.

....

The guy who invented the fold out bed died. He would have died in his sleep but the hard metal bar was digging into his back.

....

The guy who invented IQ tests died when his car, going south at ten miles and hour, was hit by a train, going north at 60 miles an hour.

....

I did a free charity gig for the Reincarnation Society. Ah, what the hell, you only live once.

....

If fitness is so good, how come you never see a jogger smiling?

....

I was never much of an athlete. When I was a kid, I played little league footy and my dad was the coach. Half way through the season he traded me to another family.

....

I just had my appendix removed. There was nothing wrong with it. I just did it as a warning to the other organs to shape up or out they go.

....

I said to my psychiatrist, 'I think I'm a dog'. He told me to get off the couch.

....

I was on a train, sitting on a newspaper, and a guy comes over and says, 'Are you reading that?' I said 'Yeah', then stood up, turned the page and sat down again.

....

It was so windy today that Advanced Hair were selling chin straps.

....

I told a guy I was getting married and he asked if I'd picked a date yet. I didn't know you could bring a date to your own wedding.

....

Women are brilliant. Every woman knows how to do the weirdest things right from the start. Every woman knows how to do that Hindu head wrap with the towel after a shower. A cyclone couldn't blow that thing off their heads. Ever seen a guy try to do that? We look like a drunk Iraqi soldier.

....

Sometimes women look at men's bodies like we're meat.

'Look at that boy. That's prime rib fillet right there.'

My body is like the part they make hot dogs out of.

....

The government has just approved pills that make you lose weight by making you feel full. The recommended dose is 5000 pills three times a day.

....

My Friend is a school teacher but he hates his job. Sometimes he would call in sick to work and just read the back of the cold and flu box verbatim.

'So what's the matter with you Joe?'

And he'd be like, 'Um, I have symptoms such as a runny nose, flu, cough, umm, I may cause drowsiness and I, umm, have to keep out of the reach of children.

....

Once we lived in a mobile home. There are advantages to living in a mobile home. One time, it caught on fire, and we met the fire department half way there.

....

It's been over a year since Jimmy Barnes sang at the Grand Final, and my cat still won't come out from behind the couch.

....

You know when they have a fishing show on TV? They catch the fish and then let it go. They don't want to eat the fish, they just want to make it late for something.

....

After you live in the city for a long time, you become oblivious to everything. You just don't notice things anymore. I sat in a coffee shop and drank half a cup of coffee before I noticed there was lipstick on the cup. And there was chewing gum wrapped up in the napkin. I must have been sitting on that woman's lap for an hour.

....

I'm terrified of being trapped in a folding bed. I'm a claustropedic.

....

The problem with the designated driver program is that it's not a fun job. So if you get the job, have fun with it. At the end of the night, drop them off at the wrong houses.

....

You know you're getting old when the candles cost more than the cake.

....

I hope that next time I move I get a really easy phone number. Something like 9999 9999. I'd say, 'Sweet'. Then when someone asks what my phone number is, I'd say, just press 9 for a while. And when I answer you'll know you've pressed 9 enough.

....

There's a lot of self-help tapes out there. I bought one called, 'How to deal with disappointment'. I got it home and the box was empty.

....

I think the most beautiful sunset I ever saw was on pages 4 and 5 of 'The book of sunsets'.

....

Don't you wish there was knob on your TV to turn up the intelligence? There's one for brightness, but that doesn't do it.

....

My dad always told me I could be anything I wanted to be when I grew up within reason. When I asked him what he meant by 'within reason', he said, 'You ask a lot of questions for a factory worker'.

I've got three kids, all by accident. We've had one using the pill, one using a condom, and one using an IUD. I don't know what happened to that IUD but I have my suspicions because the kid picks up Foxtel.

There will be a rain dance Friday night, weather permitting.

As I felt the soft cool mud squishing between my toes I thought, 'Man, these are not very good shoes'.

Ever notice when you blow in a dog's face he gets mad at you but when you take him in the car he puts his head out of the window.

The one good thing about trying comedy;
if you fail, nobody laughs at you.

....

I opened up tub of yoghurt and
underneath the lid it said, 'Please
try again', because Yoplait are running
a competition I didn't know about,
but I thought I might have opened
the yoghurt wrong. Or maybe Yoplait
were trying to inspire me. Giving me a
message of encouragement. 'C'mon
Marty, don't give up. Please try again.'
A message of inspiration from your
friends at Yoplait. Fruit on the bottom,
hope on top.

....

Kids don't need expensive new toys to have
fun. In my day we'd have just as much fun
getting into my dad's car and letting off the
handbrake and just seeing how far the car
would go before it hit something.

....

In my next life, I hope I come back as a
parrot, because I already know quite a
few words.

....

When I found the wallet on the road,
I started wondering about the guy who
owned it. Who was he? Was it David Bowler
of Unit 2, 75 Marlon Street, Kew, like the
license said, or was it someone else?
And what was he going to spend his
$325 on? About a week later, I started
wondering about the wallet guy again.
What was he like? And where was he
going to spend his $5?

....

I was an ugly kid. My father and I walked
out of the pet shop, and the alarm went off.

....

I was sitting at the lights and I was eating
a banana. On a traffic light green means
go, and yellow means wait. On a banana
it's just the opposite. On a banana,
green means wait, yellow means go,
and red means, 'Where the fuck did you
get that banana?'

....

I hope I never do anything to bring shame
on myself, my family, or my other family.

....

Dolphin-safe tuna. That's great if you're a dolphin, but what if you're a tuna? Somewhere there's a tuna flopping around the deck of a ship going, 'What about me? I'm not cute enough for you?'

....

Why pay five dollars for a bookmark? Use the five dollars as a bookmark.

....

I broke up with my girlfriend. She moved in with another guy, and I draw the line at that.

....

I was walking through the park when I had a very bad asthma attack. These three asthmatics attacked me. I know, I should have heard them hiding.

....

In my manual on deep sea survival, if a shark attacks you're supposed to poke it in the eye. Who wrote that? The three stooges?

....

I haven't slept for three days. Because that would be too long.

....

I'm heavily in debt at the moment.
My goal now is to just be broke. I just want
to get back to zero. I'll have nothing but
that will be something. I'll leave it to my
kids. 'See all this? None of this is all yours.'

....

A new report says that raw eggs may
have salmonella, and could be unsafe.
The latest government theory says that
it wasn't the fall that killed Humpty
Dumpty – he was dead before he hit
the ground.

....

We took the Concorde. It was cool.
It travels at twice the speed of sound,
which is fun, except you can't hear the
movie until an hour after you land.

....

Police arrested two kids yesterday, one
was drinking battery acid, and the other
was eating fireworks. They charged one
and let the other one off.

....

Most dentists' chairs go up and down.
But the one that I was in went back and
forwards. I thought, 'This is unusual.'
The dentist said to me 'Mr. Fields,
get out of the filing cabinet.'

....

Last week I helped my friend stay put. It's
a lot easier than helping someone move.
I went over to his house and made sure he
didn't start loading stuff into a truck.

....

Have you seen those paintings of dogs
playing poker? There's nothing funny
about that. There's nothing cute about
animals with gambling problems. If you
look closely at the painting you can see
those dogs are tense, because most of
them are playing with money they can't
afford to lose. And sadder still, it takes
seven of their dollars to make one of ours.

....

At golf, I don't rent a cart. I don't need
one. Where I hit the ball, I can use
public transport.

....

I went to the doctor's to get a physical examination for some life insurance. After the results, all they would cover me for was fire and theft.

....

I think doctors are crooks. Why do you think when they write out a prescription, only the doctor and the chemist can read it? Because they all say the same thing: 'I got my money, you get yours.'

....

I bought a box of animal crackers. There was a warning on it that said, 'Do not eat if seal is broken.' So I opened up the box and sure enough...

....

I eat too much fast food, I've become a fast food connoisseur. I was in line at Maccas and the guy in front of me orders a fillet 'o fish and a strawberry shake, and I'm like, 'Hmmph, a red shake? With seafood?'

....

I think Bigfoot is blurry. That's the problem. It's not the photographer's fault. Big foot is blurry.

Which I think is extra-scary. There's a large out of focus monster roaming the countryside. 'Run, he's fuzzy. Get out of here.'

....

At the gym, my favourite machine is the vending machine.

....

I've taken up meditation. At least it's better than sitting around doing nothing.

....

Kmart announced it's laying off 1500 employees because of falling sales. Smart move. Now the only place those people will be able to afford to shop will be Kmart.

....

I go to a very fancy gym. They have a spiral stairmaster.

....

As a kid, when I misbehaved sometimes
Dad would bury me in the backyard.
Only up to the waist, but you get dizzy
with all the blood rushing to your head.

....

I saw one of those mime performers
busking in the mall. He's doing that famous
mime routine where he pretends to be
trapped in a box. He's pretty good and,
thank God, it turns out he wasn't really
trapped in a box. He was only miming.
So I went over and mimed putting a dollar
in his hat.

....

Universal Pictures had to push back
the filming of the third *Babe* movie.
Apparently the caterers made a terrible,
terrible mistake.

....

Here's a tip for the guys. Don't mess
around inside your girlfriend's handbag.
She's like, 'What happened to my eyeliner
pencil?' 'Um, the phone rang and I had to
write down a message and I couldn't find
a pen. It's just a pencil. I'll go replace it.'

$38 and a decent command of the French
language later...

....

My gym has 500 gram weights. If you're using 500 gram weights, how the hell do you carry that towel around with you? What are you trying to do? Pump up so you can open your mail?

....

Dad didn't want to send me to a catholic school because the teachers hit the kids, so he sent me to a high school, where the kids hit the teachers.

....

The word 'Aerobics' comes from the Greek 'aero' meaning 'ability to' and 'bics' meaning 'withstand tremendous boredom'.

....

At high school I studied legal studies. I learned about the third tort of common law. That's the one concerned with search and seizure. For example if my mother had have searched my room, she would have had a seizure.

....

My ex-wife and I get together and talk about the good old day.

....

We split because we couldn't have kids.
It was in our lease.

....

Times are tough. I did a corporate
mini-golf day.

....

Have you seen those DVDs you can get
of a fireplace? They're great except if
you're drunk. I don't know if you've seen
what happens when you throw a log into a
50-inch plasma. Ironically it started a fire.

....

Golden eagles have an interesting way
of mating, where they connect in the air
while flying at 100 k's an hour and then
they start dropping and they don't stop
dropping until the act is completed. So it's
not uncommon that they both fall all the
way to the ground, hit the ground and both
of them die. That's how committed they
are to this. I thought to myself, don't we
feel like wimps for stopping to answer the
phone? I don't know about you, but if I'm
one of these two birds, you're getting close
to the ground, I would seriously consider
faking it.

....

Normal is getting dressed in clothes that you buy for work and driving through traffic in a car that you are still paying for – in order to get to the job you need to pay for the clothes and the car, and the house you leave vacant all day so you can afford to live in it.

....

The Victorian Government has shown us they still have a sense of humour by diverting funds from hospitals to pay for a clown school. The Premier said, 'Victoria has a long history of funding clowns. These kids have got some big shoes to fill. For a start they all have to travel to school in one car.'

....

Qantas staff were trying to get a 2% pay rise to try and keep up with inflation. Qantas CEO Alan Joyce got a two million dollar pay rise to try and keep up with Richard Brandson.

....

A pet census was conducted by the government this week. Pets can either complete the survey online or do it on the paper.

....

The commissioner of taxation is asking for a 58% pay rise taking his wage to $800,000. Who's going to be brave enough to say no? Maybe he'd be willing to negotiate. 'You want 800 grand to run the tax office? That seems a little high. How much for cash?'

....

A major city sewer was blocked with excrement and causing horrible smells to shoppers. City West Water sent a guy down to clear the blockage armed only with a shovel and the short straw he drew.

....

Crown Casino has said there is no evidence that limiting pokies to a dollar per spin would affect the gambling problem. 'The losses would still be as big,' the casino said. 'All the change would do is shift the losses from them to us.'

....

A new psychological survey has told us the three best ways to beat stress include getting a dog, going to church and making love. The survey also suggests that if you really want to avoid stress, don't do all three at once.

....

A 15-month-old boy couldn't get a grip on the toy he wanted in one of those 'pick up a toy using the claw' machines so he climbed up the toy chute and got stuck inside the glass case. Firemen finally got him out three hours, $72 and nine SpongeBobs later.

....

A Queensland plumber called police after he found a stash of cocaine in a toilet he bought at a secondhand hardware sale. Police said it was a whole new slant on the term 'Plumber's Crack.'

....

I told my wife I needed more space so she locked me outside.

....

I went to the 50th reunion of my kindergarten. I didn't want to go, because I've put on, like, 90 kilos.

....

When I go to a restaurant I always ask the manager, 'Give me a table near a waiter'.

....

I worry that the person who thought up
Muzak may be thinking up something else.

....

Science has found the gene for shyness.
They would have found it earlier, but it was
hiding behind a couple of other genes.

....

They say that kissing a smoker is like
licking an ashtray, which is a good thing
to remember when you're home alone
with an ashtray.

....

My cousin wanted to be an actress.
She never made it but she does live in
a caravan, so she sort of got half way.
It's like she's an actress. She's just
never called to the set.

....

In school I was never the class clown;
I was more the class trapeze artist.
I was always getting suspended.

....

My pet goldfish got a bladder infection.
I didn't know it was urinating 37 times
a day until the fish tank overflowed.

....

At the 7-11, there's a sign that says, 'Please pay with your smallest bill', so I gave the guy the little white one-dollar bill from my monopoly set. The cops picked me up a block away but it was OK. I also had the 'get out of jail free' card.

....

I was a bank teller. That was a great job. I was bringing home $450,000 a week.

....

At the age of fifty our body is supposedly slowing down. I haven't noticed that, unless what slows down first is our ability to notice things.

....

If you've only ever read the word 'Catholic' not heard it said, you might think it means someone who's addicted to cats.

....

Our teacher at school tried to make the lessons apply to the real world. She'd hand back a test and say, 'Suzie, you got 80, which is a B, and also the speed limit on Nepean Highway. Uh oh, Marty, you got the speed limit on Little Bourke Street.'

....

I know a lot about cars. I can look at a car's headlights and tell you exactly which way it's coming from.

....

You may have seen my Grandfather in the news. When he was 101 years old he ran the fifteen hundred metres and set a record for people over 100 years old. But now they're protesting the record because when he started the race he was only 98.

....

I saw an ad in the paper: 'Summer sale – Last week'. Why advertise? I already missed it. Why rub it in?

....

The biggest marketing disaster in history was Campbell's Soup For One. They might as well have called it 'Cream of Loser'. Open can, add tears.

....

I don't wear a watch because I want my arms to weigh the same.

....

The oldest man in the world died yesterday at the age of 112. The cause of death, say the doctors, was being 112.

....

I'm sure those new alcoholic lemonade drinks and 'alcopops' are aimed at kids. Even Heinz has come out with strained banana daiquiris.

....

I remember on my 18th birthday, my parents tried to surprise me with a car, but they missed.

....

My grandfather was so old his blood type was discontinued.

....

I think camping is nature's way of promoting the motel business.

....

I've never understood why women love cats. Cats are independent, they don't listen, they don't come in when you call, they like to stay out all night, and when they're home they like to be left alone and sleep. In other words, every quality women hate in a man, they love in a cat.

....

The government say that 12% of people haven't returned their census forms. How do they know that?

....

Most kids threaten at some stage to run away from home. This is the only thing that keeps some parent going.

....

I remember one hotel I stayed in had a sign out the front, 'You'll feel like you're at home.' Half way through the night they started banging on my door, yelling, 'When are you going to move out and find a place of your own?'

....

I can't throw anything away. I'm such a hoarder that when I lost twenty kilos, I couldn't throw away my fat clothes. I just bagged them up and put them in the garage, next to my dead brother's clothes, next to my dead brother.

....

I used to work in a false advertising agency.

....

Computers let you make more mistakes faster than any invention in history with the possible exception of balaclavas and tequila.

....

I don't see the point in testing cosmetics on rabbits because they're already cute.

....

Fugitive drug kingpin Amado Carrillo Fuentes died after nine hours of cosmetic surgery and liposuction. Or as it's known in show business, natural causes.

....

I think they should put expiration dates on clothes so we men will know when they go out of style.

....

I got robbed. I rang the insurance company. They asked me what policy I had. I told them I had fire and theft. They said that's no good. I should have has fire OR theft. I'm only covered if the guy robs me while the place is burning down.

....

My doctor ran some tests. I went back for the results. He said 'I've got some good news and some bad news. What do you want to hear first?' I said, 'The good news.' He said, 'But I could be wrong...'

....

In Vegas, I stayed at the Luxor, which is that big pyramid. And the problem with the Luxor is that if you lose all your money and you jump out of your hotel room window, you don't die. You just slide all the way down the side of the building making a squeaky noise.

....

Honesty is the key to relationships. If you can fake that, you're in.

....

They have luggage shops at airports. Who forgets their suitcase? Have you ever seen a guy with an armload of clothes at the airport going, 'I can't help feeling I've forgotten something...'

....

I went to a self-help group for compulsive talkers called On and On Anon.

....

I asked this girl to come back to my place for coffee. She said, 'No. When I drink coffee, I can't sleep.' I said, 'I'm the opposite. When I sleep, I can't drink coffee.'

....

Have you heard about those mystery flights? Return airfares for $59. The only restriction is they don't tell you what city you're going to. So basically you become your luggage.

....

My friends all tell me I have an intimacy problem. But they don't really know me.

....

I intend to live forever. So far, so good.

....

One of the first things they teach you at driving school is where to put your hands on the wheel – at 10 o'clock and 2 o'clock. I put mine at 9.45 and 2.15. It gives me an extra half-hour to get where I'm going.

....

I'm single by choice. Not my choice...

....

I finally saw the movie *Crouching Tiger, Hidden Dragon*. I was disappointed.
I didn't see any tigers or dragons, but then I realised they were all crouching and hiding.

....

A couple got married on our flight.
They had the whole service on the plane. It didn't go that well, though. All your life you dream about walking down the aisle, and when the big moment comes, you're stuck behind the drinks trolley.

....

My mother was a clean freak. She vacuumed so much the guy downstairs went bald.

....

I said to the pilot as we got on, 'Do these planes crash much?' He said, 'No, just the once.'

....

To celebrate the invention of sandpaper, Kmart are offering 50% off their home brand toilet paper.

....

Here's some advice. At a job interview tell them you're willing to commit 110%. Unless of course the job is for a statistician, because you'll look like an idiot.

....

I admit it, I'm a hypochondriac. But I control it with a placebo. Actually, I'm addicted to placebos. I'd give them up but it wouldn't do any good.

....

My Uncle was thrown out of a mime show for having a seizure. They thought he was heckling.

....

I asked my mother if I was adopted. She said, 'Not yet, but we placed an ad.'

....

The movie *Dude, Where's My Car?* did so well, they're making a sequel, 'Oh, there it is.'

....

The song, 'If I had a hammer' is geared toward people who don't have a hammer. Maybe before I had a hammer, I thought I'd hammer in the morning and hammer in the evening. But once you finally get a hammer, you find you don't really hammer as much as you thought you would.

....

America have got the stealth plane, the invisible plane. What good is an invisible plane? The enemy looks at their radar and are, like, 'Well there's no aircraft here. But something's weird because there's two little guys in a sitting position at forty thousand feet.'

....

My neighbour asked if he could use my lawnmower. I told him of course he could as long as he didn't take it out of my yard.

....

George Bush wasn't too smart. He submitted to a drug test but before he went in he wrote the answers on his hand.

....

First the doctor told me the good news:
I was going to have a disease named
after me.

....

Keith Richards doesn't strike me as a
morning person.

....

I can't believe the luge is such a respected
event at the Winter Olympics. They don't
do anything. Luge strategy: Lie flat and try
not to die.

....

The U.S. Air Force has just bought a
squadron of new bombers. Why do they
need new bombers? What was wrong with
their old ones? Have the people they've
been bombing over the years
been complaining?

....

I admire the Pope. I have a lot of respect
for anyone who can tour without an album.

....

Prince William was busted for smoking
marijuana. Apparently 'Your Highness'
is not just an expression.

....

Whenever I see people who make balloon animals for a living, I always think of their relatives and how disappointed they must be.

....

My friend is a heavy smoker. His teeth are so yellow when he smiles, cars get ready to stop.

....

In Melbourne you haven't had enough coffee until you can thread a sewing machine while it's running.

....

I worked at the wedding of the guy who owns 'Mr. Antenna'. Terrible wedding but what a reception!

....

My friend's dog is cross between a Chihuahua and a Great Dane. It has the head of a Great Dane and the body of a Chihuahua. The dog has to walk everywhere backwards dragging his enormous oversized head along the ground on a roller skate.

....

Darth Vader says to Luke Skywalker, 'Luke, I know what you're getting for Christmas', and Luke says, 'How, Father?' and Darth Vader says, 'I felt your presents.'

....

This priest gets pulled over. The cop smells booze on his breath. He spots a wine bottle on the floor of the car. He asks the priest if he's been drinking. The priest says, 'No only this bottle of water down here.' The cop says, 'Well how come I can smell wine on your breath?' The priest says, 'Oh my Lord, he's done it again!'

....

At a job interview at a cinema:

INTERVIEWER: 'So what makes you think you'd be a good usher?'

ME: (I pick up my resumé and rip it a little bit.)

INTERVIEWER: Nice.

....

A brain walks into a bar and orders a beer. The barman says, 'Sorry buddy, but I can see you're already out of your head.'

....

I belong to a gym. Well let me rephrase that; I don't belong there, but I go.

....

Two aircraft mechanics finish work at Tullamarine and one says, 'Hey let's go get a beer', and the other says, 'Actually, why don't we try drinking jet fuel? I hear it tastes like whiskey, and you don't get a hangover in the morning' So they drink about two litres of it each. It tastes great and they have a great night.

The next morning one of the mechanics rings the other and says, 'How do you feel?'

The other says, 'I feel fine'.

The first one says, 'Me too. No hangover. Just one thing, have you farted yet?' The second one says, 'No'.

'Well don't. I'm calling from Perth'.

....

Have you seen the weather channel on cable? 24 hours a day of weather. We had something like that when I was a kid. We called it a 'window'.

....

Canada is a country without a cuisine. Seriously, when was the last time you went out for Canadian?

....

Two goldfish are in a tank and one says to the other, 'I knew we shouldn't have joined the army.'

....

It was my Uncle's funeral and the pallbearers were carrying the coffin out from the church. As they got to the top of the church stairs they bumped into a pillar and one of them heard a moan from inside the casket. They opened it up and found that my uncle was still alive. God be praised. He lived for another ten years at home, under the constant care of my Auntie, cooking for him, changing his nappies, wiping up his mess, giving him medicine before he finally died. Another funeral was held for him in the very same church and as the pallbearers were carrying the casket out of the church, my Auntie called out, 'Watch out for that frickin' pillar!'

....

The worst soccer player in history was Cinderella. She ran away from the ball and had a pumpkin for a coach.

How do you get a guitarist to turn down the volume? Put sheet music in front of him.

I went to the fortune teller at the carnival. I went into her tent and sat down. She was looking into her crystal ball. She said 'I can see a tall dark stranger with a giant round head'. I said 'That's my reflection'.

My friend has a subscription to a running magazine. Running! A subscription! I mean maybe there's enough to say about running for one edition but a subscription, he's sending his money in month after month and they keep sending him new issues. They eventually wrote him a letter. 'Look, there's really not much more we can tell you. Um, keep running.'

I took a physical for some life insurance. All they would cover me for was fire and theft.

....

What's the big deal about compulsory drug testing? I know some guys who'd be willing to test any drug they can come up with.

....

I was so ugly I didn't have plastic surgery, I had plastic explosive surgery. They had to blast the ugly off.

....

Have you been to the gym lately? Some of those guys there are a bit over developed. Here's a tip, if your neck's as wide as your head, take a day off.

....

If I ever had twins, I'd use one for parts.

....

At night, men won't turn on the bathroom light to pee. We pee by sonar. We just keep peeing till we hear water.

....

If you want to be a world leader you have to be committed. When you make a decision you can't waiver in any way. You'd never see Ghandi during a hunger strike sneaking into the kitchen in the middle of the night. 'Ghandi... what are you doing down there?' 'I... um... thought I heard a burglar and I was going to hit him over the head with this big bowl of potato salad.'

....

My ex-wife was a comic too. We'd been together a while and had come up with a lot of material together, so when we got divorced, the settlement was, like, 'OK, you get the joke about the house, I'll have the joke about the car.'

'What about the kids?'

'Keep 'em, they're not funny.'

....

In school, I just couldn't pass a maths test. I couldn't pass a drug test either. There may be a link there.

....

Meatloaf is planning to release a Christmas album. This is so Santa has something to give the naughty kids.

....

A man is in hospital after swallowing 67 coins for a bet. Doctors say so far, no change.

....

Scientists at the CSIRO say there's more bacteria on bank notes than on a toilet so we need to stop paying our plumbers in cash.

....

In business news internet company Yahoo! have just sacked hundreds of employees. That's gotta be a tough dismissal letter to get. 'Dear Barbara. You no longer work here. Yahoo!'

....

A world eating champion has passed away at the age of 77. Some of his records include eating 27 chickens, 55 bowls of fried rice and 12 kilos of ham. Relatives say his remains will be buried in a takeaway container.

....

A truck rolled on the Gold Coast Motorway, spilling its twelve-tonne load of onions onto the road. According to a witness, no one was hurt, but everyone was crying.

....

U.S. cops were on the scene of an attack at Hollywood Boulevard in California which is famous for its celebrity impersonators. Police are looking for a Charlie Chaplin who indecently assaulted a Marilyn Monroe. The only witness was a Harpo Marx, and he's not talking.

....

Knock knock...

Who's there?

Grandad.

QUICK, STOP THE CREMATION!

....

DYSON VACUUM: I can pick up anything.

ME: Great. My daughter finishes dance class in the city at 5.30. Good luck.

....

COP: This is a ticket for drunk and
disorderly behaviour.

ME: Can I have another one? I'd like
to bring a guest.

....

A vegan said to me people who sell meat
are gross.

I said people who sell fruit and vegetables
are grocer.

....

I took my cat to the vet yesterday and,
once again, she 'forgot' her wallet.

....

Even though I was nervous I went skydiving
today. This guy strapped himself to me,
and before I knew it we'd jumped out of
the plane. As we plummeted towards the
earth he said, 'So, how long have you been
an instructor?'

....

I can't help feeling that the Grand Prix
cars wouldn't have to go so fast if they
just left earlier.

....

I don't get why they have cooking shows on TV. I can't smell it, I can't eat it, I can't taste it. At the end of the show they hold it up to the camera. 'Well, here it is. You can't have any. Goodnight.'

....

I want to knock down a wall to create another bathroom in our house but our neighbours are objecting because at the moment it's their bathroom.

....

I'm at the gym and I see lots of people on the exercise bikes put a water bottle in that hole where the Pringles are supposed to go.

....

A guy on the street stopped me and asked if I could spare two minutes for heart disease research.

I said, 'Sure, but I don't think we'll get much done.'

....

My favourite machine at the casino is the change machine. It's great. You put in $50, you get $50. You put in $100, you get $100. I feel sorry for the guy who owns it though. Every night at closing time he must be like, 'Damn, I broke even again!'

....

I asked the guy at the 7Eleven, 'How much are Cherry Ripes?'

He said, 'They're two for $3.'

I said, 'How much is one?'

He said 'They're $2.'

I said, 'I'll have the other one.'

....

Toothpicks are great for when you have something stuck in your teeth but you also want something else stuck in your teeth.

....

I went to an auction and bought a really cheap signed photo of Ronnie Corbett.

My mate got a really cheap signed photo of Ronnie Barker.

So it's a good buy from me and a good buy from him.

....

ABOUT THE AUTHOR

Marty Fields is one of Australia's most popular and versatile performers, a finely tuned and in-demand corporate comedian, Host/MC, actor and musician. The son of Aussie icons Maurie Fields and Val Jellay, Marty was introduced to the entertainment industry at an early age. Originally an actor and musician, he graduated from the esteemed Melba Conservatorium then began his standup comedy career in 1983.

He is the author of *Takeaway Jokes* (1999), *Funny Things* (2010), *Short Jokes for Tall People* (2017) and *Funny is Still Funny* (2019).